AF349299

IMO

OLYMPIAD WORKBOOK

INTERNATIONAL MATHEMATICS OLYMPIAD

- **01** Learning Objectives
- **02** Multiple Choice Questions
- **03** HOTS (Achievers Section)
- **04** Model Test Paper
- **05** Answer Keys and Solutions
- **06** OMR Answer Sheet

Published by:

V&S PUBLISHERS

F-2/16, Ansari road, Daryaganj, New Delhi-110002
☎ 23240026, 23240027 • *Fax:* 011-23240028
✉ info@vspublishers.com • ⊕ www.vspublishers.com

 **Online Brandstore: amazon.in/vspublishers**

Regional Office : Hyderabad
5-1-707/1, Brij Bhawan (Beside Central Bank of India Lane)
Bank Street, Koti, Hyderabad - 500 095
☎ 040-24737290
✉ vspublishershyd@gmail.com

Follow us on:   

BUY OUR BOOKS FROM: AMAZON FLIPKART

© Copyright: *V&S* PUBLISHERS
ISBN 978-81-977325-7-7
New Edition

PUBLISHER'S NOTE

V&S Publishers has carved a significant niche in the publishing industry over the last decade, having successfully published more than 1000 titles across 9 languages spanning over 50 subject categories. Being known for the quality of content, we have built a reputation of excellence and reliability. We have consistently delivered **"Value & Substance"** to our readers, through a wide range of titles across a variety of genres covering school books, fiction and non-fiction that caters to different people from every section of the society.

The **Olympiad Guidebooks for classes 1-10** across all subjects, launched almost a decade ago, under the **GEN X Imprint**, became a go-to-source for the school students in no time, owing to their invaluable and substantive content written in a guidebook pattern,.

Having successfully sold a million copies of the same and in response to demand by both students as well as shopkeepers nationwide; we now present before you our newly launched **Olympiad Workbook Series**, designed for **classes 1-10 across 4 subjects**.

The workbooks are meticulously curated by a team of experienced educators, researchers and subject matter experts, edited by professionals and peer reviewed by teachers. The team has poured its efforts and expertise into creating a crisp and concise workbook which will help and guide the students to the path of success in Olympiad exams. The **MCQs** identified will not only help in scoring top marks in Olympiads but also inculcate a sense of deeper understanding of the subject, by way of solving **HOTS** and referring to complete solutions at the end of the book.

Here we present our new release– **OLYMPIAD WORKBOOK (IMO) CLASS–4** having following features:

- ☞ Based on the latest syllabi
- ☞ MCQs with comprehensive coverage of topics
- ☞ HOTS Questions liberally included
- ☞ A dedicated chapter on logical reasoning
- ☞ Model test paper for thorough practice
- ☞ Sample OMR sheet for real time simulation

We have made sure through our best efforts, that this workbook strictly follows the latest syllabi and patterns of the Olympiad Examination.

As **V&S Publishers** continuously strive to enhance the readability and maintain the credibility of our academic publications, we seek the support of our valuable readers in influencing and enriching the lives of future generations of students.

P.S. While every care has been taken to ensure the correctness of the content, if you come across any error, howsoever minor, do not hesitate to discuss with teachers while pointing that out to us in no uncertain terms.

We wish you all the best for your exams!

DISTINCTIVE FEATURES

01 — Learning Objectives

They list the whole chapter as subtopics, helping the teachers to guide children in a step-by-step manner.

02 — Multiple Choice Questions

MCQs act as an excellent learning aid, helping you to understand and work on your mistakes.

03 — HOTS (Achievers Section)

The High Order Thinking Questions aim to help the student to solve Application-based questions and gain practical understanding of the subject.

04 — Model Test Paper

Model test paper are provided at the end of each book, which help the student to test the knowledge which they have gained after thorough reading of all chapters.

05 — Answer Key

Detailed Answer Key along with explanations aid the pupil to indentify, understand the mistakes they make during the course of Olympiad preparation.

CONTENTS

NUMBER SENSE

LEARNING OBJECTIVES

➤ Number Names
➤ 5-digit and 6-digit Numbers
➤ Place Value and Face Value

➤ Comparing Numbers
➤ Successor and Predecessor
➤ Ascending and Descending Order

MULTIPLE CHOICE QUESTIONS

1. 99,999 is the greatest _____ digit number.
   (A) 5   (B) 4
   (C) 3   (D) 2

2. Place value of 5 in 5,43,621 is ________.
   (A) 500000   (B) 5000
   (C) 50   (D) 5

3. Smallest 6-digit number is ________.
   (A) 10,0001   (B) 1,00,000
   (C) 9,99,999   (D) 99,999

4. 300000 + 20000 + 4000 + 200 + 2 = _____
   (A) 3,24,202   (B) 3,42,222
   (C) 2,34,222   (D) 3,22,432

5. Ones period includes.
   (A) Hundreds
   (B) Thousands
   (C) Ten thousands
   (D) Lakhs

6. The difference between the place values of '9' and '3' in 43549 is _____.
   (A) 2991   (B) 291
   (C) 2990   (D) 29900

7. Smallest six-digit number having 2 at hundred's place is _____.
   (A) 321201   (B) 301761
   (C) 331201   (D) 300111

8. Pick the odd one out.
   (A) Hundreds   (B) Tens
   (C) Ones   (D) Lakhs

9. We use ________ to separate the periods.
   (A) Comma   (B) Full stop
   (C) Brackets   (D) Hyphen

10. 4,37,283 is a __________ number.
    (A) 4-digit   (B) 5-digit
    (C) 6-digit   (D) 7-digit

11. The descending order of 12432, 12342, 12234, 12324 is _____.
    (A) 12324, 12432, 13342, 12234
    (B) 12432, 12342, 12324, 12234
    (C) 12234, 12324, 12342, 12432
    (D) 12432, 12324, 12342, 12234

12. Ten lakhs comes in ________ period.
    (A) Thousands
    (B) Lakhs
    (C) Ones
    (D) Hundreds

13. Pick odd one out.
    (A) 6, 34, 231
    (B) 1, 34, 345
    (C) 1, 34, 655
    (D) 23,456

14. 1 hundred thousands = _________
    (A) 1 Lakh
    (B) 10 Lakh
    (C) 100 Lakh
    (D) 1000 Lakh

15. Ninety-two thousands three hundred forty-five is same as _________.
    (A) 92, 435
    (B) 90, 453
    (C) 92, 145
    (D) 92, 345

16. 3,44,567 has _____________ lakhs.
    (A) 3
    (B) 4
    (C) 5
    (D) 6

17. What is the estimated value of 735 nearest to 100?
    (A) 730
    (B) 700
    (C) 800
    (D) 750

18. What is the expanded form of 39,524?
    (A) 30000 + 9000 + 500 + 20 + 4
    (B) 3000 + 900 + 500 + 20 + 4
    (C) 30000 + 9000 + 500 + 20
    (D) 30000 + 9000 + 20 + 4

19. If 3256 is rounded off to the nearest ___, the answer will be 3000.
    (A) Tens
    (B) Thousands
    (C) Hundreds
    (D) None of these

20. Difference between smallest 5-digit number and smallest 4-digit number is _________.
    (A) 90000
    (B) 1000
    (C) 9000
    (D) 10000

21. The price of a car is 411140. What is the rounded off price of the car to the nearest 100?
    (A) 411130
    (B) 411100
    (C) 411200
    (D) 411150

22. The costs of three computers are ₹ 25,351, ₹ 25,400, and ₹ 30,251. What is the least cost of the computer?
    (A) ₹ 29,451
    (B) ₹ 25,400
    (C) ₹ 30,251
    (D) ₹ 25,351

23. Ravi has got five thousand nine hundreds rupees in a lottery. What is the figure value of this amount?
    (A) 590
    (B) 5900
    (C) 5090
    (D) 5009

24. A city has a population of 894710. Rounded off the population 894710 to the nearest 1000 is.
    (A) 894000
    (B) 894700
    (C) 895000
    (D) 894600

25. Sneha has 4 slips containing these four numbers.

    93543   72411   23456   43517

    She wants to know which one out of these numbers contains 4 at tens place. Help her to find it.
    (A) 72411
    (B) 93543
    (C) 43517
    (D) 23456

26. In a grazing field there are 50 goats, 40 deers and 10 children. How many legs are there in the field?
    (A) 200
    (B) 360
    (C) 380
    (D) 400

27. Make smallest and greatest seven-digit number and then find the difference between them.
    (A) 8999999
    (B) 9999888
    (C) 8999988
    (D) 8998899

28. 7 thousands, 3 hundreds and 3 ones is same as _______.
    (A) 7071
    (B) 7375
    (C) 10435
    (D) 7790

29. _______ thousands = 80 hundred
    (A) 8
    (B) 7
    (C) 6
    (D) 9

30. Find the place value of 9 in the difference obtained by subtracting 70 ones from 60 hundred.
    (A) 9000
    (B) 900
    (C) 90
    (D) 9

—Darken Your Choice with HB Pencil—

1. A B C D	7. A B C D	13. A B C D	19. A B C D	25. A B C D
2. A B C D	8. A B C D	14. A B C D	20. A B C D	26. A B C D
3. A B C D	9. A B C D	15. A B C D	21. A B C D	27. A B C D
4. A B C D	10. A B C D	16. A B C D	22. A B C D	28. A B C D
5. A B C D	11. A B C D	17. A B C D	23. A B C D	29. A B C D
6. A B C D	12. A B C D	18. A B C D	24. A B C D	30. A B C D

COMPUTATION OPERATION

LEARNING OBJECTIVES

➤ Roman Symbols
➤ Properties of addition
➤ Properties of Subtraction
➤ Properties of Multiplication
➤ Long Division
➤ Factors and Multiples

MULTIPLE CHOICE QUESTIONS

1. Romans used the numbers for trading and _____ .
   (A) Commerce
   (B) Finance
   (C) Law
   (D) Exporting

2. Addition is only applicable when the first symbol is __________ than the second, third.
   (A) Greater
   (B) Smaller
   (C) Equal
   (D) Greater than equal to

3. **Statement A:** When the principle of addition is used, a symbol can be used only three times.
   Statement B: When the principle of addition is used, a symbol can be used only 1 time.
   (A) A is correct
   (B) B is correct
   (C) Both are correct
   (D) Both are incorrect

4. Pick the odd one out.
   V, IV, X, XI, VIIII.
   (A) IV
   (B) XI
   (C) V
   (D) VIIII

5. Pick the odd one out.
   I, V, X, L, C, D, N.
   (A) X
   (B) I
   (C) C
   (D) N

6. The sum is always _____ than the numbers being added, except of the numbers being added is _____ .
   (A) Greater, zero
   (B) Less, zero
   (C) Greater, one
   (D) Less, one

7. If we change the order of the numbers being added, the _____ does not change.
   (A) Sum
   (B) Difference
   (C) Multiplication
   (D) Division

8. $0 + 33456 =$ _______
   (A) 0
   (B) 33456
   (C) 34346
   (D) 30456

9. If we add _____ to any number, the sum remains the same.
   (A) Zero
   (B) One
   (C) Two
   (D) Three

10. __________ is taking away some objects from a given collection.

(A) Addition
(B) Subtraction
(C) Multiplication
(D) Division

11. The result obtained after subtraction is called __________.
(A) Minuend
(B) Subtrahend
(C) Difference
(D) Sum

12. __________ is the number that is to be subtracted from.
(A) Minuend
(B) Subtrahend
(C) Difference
(D) Sum

13. Pick the odd one out.
(A) Minus
(B) Less
(C) Difference
(D) Sum

14. Multiplicand × Multiplier = ?
(A) Product
(B) Difference
(C) Sum
(D) Addend

15. Multiplication is the short form of repeated __________
(A) Multiplication
(B) Division
(C) Addition
(D) Subtraction

16. 43243 × 0 = __________
(A) 43432
(B) 0
(C) 44432
(D) 42432

17. 66 × 26 = __________
(A) 1716
(B) 1767
(C) 1765
(D) 0

18. When we share equally, we __________.
(A) Add
(B) Subtract
(C) Multiply
(D) Divide

19. The number to be divided is called the __________.
(A) Quotient
(B) Divisor
(C) Dividend
(D) Remainder

20. After dividing a number, the leftover is called __________.
(A) Quotient
(B) Divisor
(C) Dividend
(D) Remainder

21. What is the remainder when 3527 is divided by 10 ?
(A) 3
(B) 5
(C) 2
(D) 7

22. Which one of the following is a factor of 45 and not a multiple of 3?
(A) 5
(B) 9
(C) 15
(D) 7

23. Which one of the following is a multiple of 2 but not a factor of 8?
(A) 2
(B) 8
(C) 4
(D) 6

24. Which is odd one out?
(A) 26
(B) 39
(C) 65
(D) 71

25. What are the multiples of 16 between 40 and 90?
(A) 48, 64, 80
(B) 44, 64, 80
(C) 42, 66, 86
(D) 46, 68, 88

26. How would you write 251 as a Roman numeral?
    (A) XCLI
    (B) CXLI
    (C) CCLI
    (D) XXLI

27. What is the sum of 1 greatest 5-digit even number and greatest 6-digit odd number?
    (A) 1099998
    (B) 1099898
    (C) 1089880
    (D) 1099997

28. Find the difference of 14,235 from the sum of 13,243 + 13,243.
    (A) 11351
    (B) 12251
    (C) 14531
    (D) 12222

29. Multiplicand × Multiplier = ?
    (A) Product
    (B) Difference
    (C) Sum
    (D) Addend

30. When we share equally, we __________.
    (A) Add
    (B) Subtract
    (C) Multiply
    (D) Divide

Darken Your Choice with HB Pencil

1.	Ⓐ Ⓑ Ⓒ Ⓓ	7.	Ⓐ Ⓑ Ⓒ Ⓓ	13.	Ⓐ Ⓑ Ⓒ Ⓓ	19.	Ⓐ Ⓑ Ⓒ Ⓓ	25.	Ⓐ Ⓑ Ⓒ Ⓓ
2.	Ⓐ Ⓑ Ⓒ Ⓓ	8.	Ⓐ Ⓑ Ⓒ Ⓓ	14.	Ⓐ Ⓑ Ⓒ Ⓓ	20.	Ⓐ Ⓑ Ⓒ Ⓓ	26.	Ⓐ Ⓑ Ⓒ Ⓓ
3.	Ⓐ Ⓑ Ⓒ Ⓓ	9.	Ⓐ Ⓑ Ⓒ Ⓓ	15.	Ⓐ Ⓑ Ⓒ Ⓓ	21.	Ⓐ Ⓑ Ⓒ Ⓓ	27.	Ⓐ Ⓑ Ⓒ Ⓓ
4.	Ⓐ Ⓑ Ⓒ Ⓓ	10.	Ⓐ Ⓑ Ⓒ Ⓓ	16.	Ⓐ Ⓑ Ⓒ Ⓓ	22.	Ⓐ Ⓑ Ⓒ Ⓓ	28.	Ⓐ Ⓑ Ⓒ Ⓓ
5.	Ⓐ Ⓑ Ⓒ Ⓓ	11.	Ⓐ Ⓑ Ⓒ Ⓓ	17.	Ⓐ Ⓑ Ⓒ Ⓓ	23.	Ⓐ Ⓑ Ⓒ Ⓓ	29.	Ⓐ Ⓑ Ⓒ Ⓓ
6.	Ⓐ Ⓑ Ⓒ Ⓓ	12.	Ⓐ Ⓑ Ⓒ Ⓓ	18.	Ⓐ Ⓑ Ⓒ Ⓓ	24.	Ⓐ Ⓑ Ⓒ Ⓓ	30.	Ⓐ Ⓑ Ⓒ Ⓓ

FRACTIONS 

3

LEARNING OBJECTIVES

➤ Types of Fractions
➤ Lowest Form of Fractions
➤ Conversion of Fractions

➤ Addition, Subtraction, Multiplication and Division of Fractions

MULTIPLE CHOICE QUESTIONS

1. Pick the odd one out.
   (A) 3/8
   (B) 4/9
   (C) 6/13
   (D) 21/5

2. Write 31/8 as a mixed fraction.
   (A) 4
   (B) 4(7/8)
   (C) 3(1/8)
   (D) 3(7/8)

3. A fraction a/b = 1, when.
   (A) a > b
   (B) a < b
   (C) a = b
   (D) None of these

4. Convert 400 ml into L.
   (A) 4/10 L
   (B) 3/10 L
   (C) 5/10 L
   (D) 7/10 L

5. Pick the odd one out.
   (A) 2/5
   (B) 3/5
   (C) 8/20
   (D) 6/15

6. Which two fractions are equivalent?
   (A) 5/2 and 2/5
   (B) 4/3 and 8/6
   (C) 1/4 and 2/4
   (D) 2/3 and 1/3

7. Evaluate 5 2/3 − 3 1/2.
   (A) 2
   (B) 2 (7/6)
   (C) 2 (1/6)
   (D) 1 (2/5)

8. How many minutes are there in 2/3 of an hour?
   (A) 40 minutes
   (B) 50 minutes
   (C) 60 minutes
   (D) 20 minutes

9. If 1/3 + 1/6 + 1/12 = X, then X + 17/12 = ________.
   (A) 4
   (B) 3
   (C) 2
   (D) 1

10. Choose the incorrect option from the following.
    (A) 1/2 = 4/8
    (B) 1/2 = 6/12
    (C) 1/3 = 5/10
    (D) 1/3 = 5/15

11. What is the fraction used to represent the shaded parts?

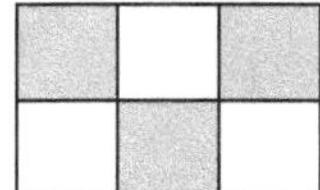 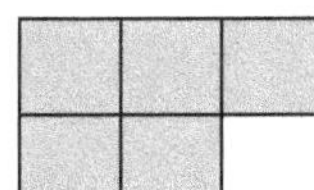

   (A) $\dfrac{3}{6} + \dfrac{4}{6}$
   (B) $\dfrac{1}{6} + \dfrac{4}{6}$
   (C) $\dfrac{3}{6} + \dfrac{5}{6}$
   (D) $\dfrac{3}{6} + \dfrac{1}{6}$

12. Reduce the given fraction to its lowest form. 9/15
    (A) 3/5
    (B) 5/3
    (C) 3/15
    (D) 5/9

Direction (13-16): Evaluate the following questions.

13. $2/5 \times 3/4 \times 5/8$

    (A) 3/8   (B) 3/7

    (C) 3/16   (D) 6/20

14. $3/8 \times 7/10 \times 5/12$

    (A) 7/64   (B) 7/81

    (C) 21/64   (D) 105/84

15. $\dfrac{\left[2\frac{1}{2}\right]}{\left[3\frac{3}{4}\right]}$

    (A) 8/75   (B) 1(1/2)

    (C) 2/3   (D) 9(3/8)

16. $[3/8]/[5/12]$

    (A) 1(1/9)   (B) 5/32

    (C) 4/5   (D) 9/10

17. The difference of shaded fraction of 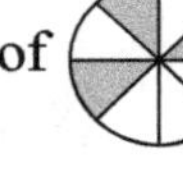 and of (figure) is ______.

    (A) $\dfrac{2}{8}$ (B) $\dfrac{3}{8}$

    (C) $\dfrac{1}{8}$ (D) $\dfrac{5}{8}$

18. How many one-sixth will make one whole?

    (A) 6   (B) 3

    (C) 2   (D) 1

19. Arrange the following in ascending order?

    $\dfrac{5}{7}, \dfrac{9}{7}, \dfrac{3}{7}, \dfrac{1}{7}, \dfrac{4}{7}, \dfrac{10}{7}$

    (A) $\dfrac{4}{7}, \dfrac{3}{7}, \dfrac{1}{7}, \dfrac{5}{7}, \dfrac{9}{7}, \dfrac{10}{7}$

    (B) $\dfrac{1}{7}, \dfrac{4}{7}, \dfrac{3}{7}, \dfrac{5}{7}, \dfrac{9}{7}, \dfrac{10}{7}$

    (C) $\dfrac{1}{7}, \dfrac{3}{7}, \dfrac{4}{7}, \dfrac{5}{7}, \dfrac{9}{7}, \dfrac{10}{7}$

    (D) $\dfrac{10}{7}, \dfrac{9}{7}, \dfrac{5}{7}, \dfrac{4}{7}, \dfrac{3}{7}, \dfrac{1}{7}$

20. Convert $3\dfrac{4}{5}$ in improper fraction.

    (A) $\dfrac{3}{5}$ (B) $\dfrac{19}{5}$

    (C) $\dfrac{4}{5}$ (D) $\dfrac{17}{5}$

21. It takes Bhola 1/2 hour to wash, comb and put on his clothes and 1/4 hour to have his breakfast. How much time does it take Bhola to be ready for office?

    (A) 3/4 hour   (B) 1 1/4 hour

    (C) 2/4 hour   (D) 1 hour

22. Out of 20 people in a line for ice cream, one-quarter want vanilla. How many people want vanilla ice cream?

    (A) 5   (B) 4

    (C) 6   (D) 8

23. Out of 8 students in Mrs. Bhatia's cart class, six-eights are in sixth grade. How many sixth graders are in Mrs. Bhatia's art class?

    (A) 1   (B) 8

    (C) 6   (D) 5

24. There are 12 berries in a bowl on the counter. Two-sixths of them are raspberries. How many raspberries are in the bowl?

    (A) 5   (B) 8

    (C) 4   (D) 6

25. Golu counted 8 students in the chair. Three-quarters of students have brown hair. How many students in the chair have brown hair?

    (A) 4   (B) 5

    (C) 6   (D) 7

26. Look at the given fractional shaded part.

Which of the following represents the same shaded fraction?

(A) 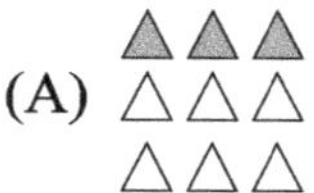

(B) 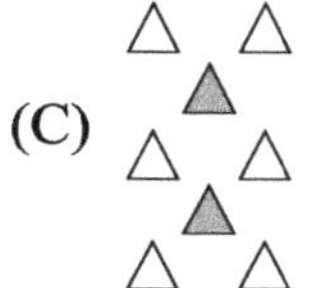

(C)

(D)

27. Which fraction number should be placed in the box so that sum of each of them is $\dfrac{15}{7}$?

$$\dfrac{3}{7}, \quad \dfrac{5}{7}, \quad \boxed{} \quad \dfrac{2}{7}, \quad \dfrac{1}{7}$$

(A) $\dfrac{4}{7}$

(B) $\dfrac{3}{7}$

(C) $\dfrac{5}{7}$

(D) None of these

28. The sum of two fractions is $\dfrac{9}{11}$. If one fraction is $\dfrac{1}{2}$. Find the other fraction.

(A) $\dfrac{7}{22}$

(B) $\dfrac{9}{22}$

(C) $\dfrac{1}{22}$

(D) $\dfrac{5}{22}$

29. Karan runs 1 km out of 4 km. Rohan runs 2 km out of 5 km and Sohan runs 3 km out of 6 km. Who runs more?

(A) Rohan

(B) Sohan

(C) Karan

(D) All run equally

30. A famous Restaurant uses the hottest peppers in its 3 Alarm Chilli. It accepts only best peppers from the produce market. Write a fraction that shows what part of this group of peppers that will be accepted.

(A) 7/12

(B) 5/12

(C) 7/24

(D) 5/24

1.	Ⓐ Ⓑ Ⓒ Ⓓ	7.	Ⓐ Ⓑ Ⓒ Ⓓ	13.	Ⓐ Ⓑ Ⓒ Ⓓ	19.	Ⓐ Ⓑ Ⓒ Ⓓ	25.	Ⓐ Ⓑ Ⓒ Ⓓ
2.	Ⓐ Ⓑ Ⓒ Ⓓ	8.	Ⓐ Ⓑ Ⓒ Ⓓ	14.	Ⓐ Ⓑ Ⓒ Ⓓ	20.	Ⓐ Ⓑ Ⓒ Ⓓ	26.	Ⓐ Ⓑ Ⓒ Ⓓ
3.	Ⓐ Ⓑ Ⓒ Ⓓ	9.	Ⓐ Ⓑ Ⓒ Ⓓ	15.	Ⓐ Ⓑ Ⓒ Ⓓ	21.	Ⓐ Ⓑ Ⓒ Ⓓ	27.	Ⓐ Ⓑ Ⓒ Ⓓ
4.	Ⓐ Ⓑ Ⓒ Ⓓ	10.	Ⓐ Ⓑ Ⓒ Ⓓ	16.	Ⓐ Ⓑ Ⓒ Ⓓ	22.	Ⓐ Ⓑ Ⓒ Ⓓ	28.	Ⓐ Ⓑ Ⓒ Ⓓ
5.	Ⓐ Ⓑ Ⓒ Ⓓ	11.	Ⓐ Ⓑ Ⓒ Ⓓ	17.	Ⓐ Ⓑ Ⓒ Ⓓ	23.	Ⓐ Ⓑ Ⓒ Ⓓ	29.	Ⓐ Ⓑ Ⓒ Ⓓ
6.	Ⓐ Ⓑ Ⓒ Ⓓ	12.	Ⓐ Ⓑ Ⓒ Ⓓ	18.	Ⓐ Ⓑ Ⓒ Ⓓ	24.	Ⓐ Ⓑ Ⓒ Ⓓ	30.	Ⓐ Ⓑ Ⓒ Ⓓ

MEASUREMENTS, TIME, CALENDERS AND MONEY

LEARNING OBJECTIVES

- ➤ Length
- ➤ Unit of currency in India
- ➤ Clock and Time
- ➤ Months, weeks and days in Calendar

MULTIPLE CHOICE QUESTIONS

Direction (1-5): Read the data given below and answer the questions:

Giraffe	Height of Giraffe
A.	438 cm
B.	620 cm
C.	286 cm
D.	526 cm

1. Which is the tallest Giraffe?
   - (A) D
   - (B) C
   - (C) B
   - (D) A

2. How much taller is Giraffe B than A?
   - (A) 180 cm
   - (B) 181 cm
   - (C) 182 cm
   - (D) 183 cm

3. How much shorter is Giraffe C than D?
   - (A) 210 cm
   - (B) 220 cm
   - (C) 230 cm
   - (D) 240 cm

4. Which is the shortest Giraffe?
   - (A) D
   - (B) C
   - (C) B
   - (D) A

5. How much taller is the tallest Giraffe than the shortest Giraffe?
   - (A) 331 cm
   - (B) 332 cm
   - (C) 333 cm
   - (D) 334 cm

6. 77 km + 2 m + 99 km 5 m = _______

   (A) 176 km 7 m

   (B) 166 km 47 m

   (C) 176 km 46 m

   (D) 176 km 40 m

7. | 1000 m | _____

   (A) | 50 m | 50 m | 800 m |

   (B) | 500 m | 250 m | 250 m |

   (C) | 250 m | 250 m | 250 m |

   (D) | 900 m | 50 m | 25 m |

8. Find the longest item from the given table.

Items	Lengths
Notebook	70 cm
Pencil	0.15 m
Pen	160 mm
Brush	20 cm

   (A) Brush

   (B) Pen

   (C) Pencil

   (D) Notebook

9. Find the difference between 65 L 534 ml and 32 L 876 ml.

   (A) 30 L 870 ml

   (B) 32 L 658 ml

   (C) 31 L 658 ml

   (D) 30 L 670 ml

10. Two pens cost ₹ 24. Find the cost of 5 such pens.

    (A) ₹ 40

    (B) ₹ 50

    (C) ₹ 60

    (D) ₹ 70

11. Add ₹ 150.60 and ₹ 140.75 and then subtract the obtained sum from ₹ 325.50.

    (A) ₹ 32.75

    (B) ₹ 34.15

    (C) ₹ 33.25

    (D) ₹ 34.75

Direction (12-15): Consider the prices of the items below to answer question.

   Apple --------- ₹ 180 per kg

   Pen --------- ₹ 8 per piece

   Eraser ------- ₹ 5 for 2 erasers

   Chocolates ------- ₹ 15 for 3 chocolates

12. Ankit wants to buy half kg apples and one chocolate. The total amount he needs to pay is _______.

    (A) ₹ 85

    (B) ₹ 95

    (C) ₹ 90

    (D) ₹ 105

13. If Bunny wants to buy one pen and 3 erasers, how much he needs to pay?

    (A) ₹ 13

    (B) ₹ 15

    (C) ₹ 15.50

    (D) ₹ 16.25

14. One kg apples can be bought for ₹ 180 and two chocolates can be bought for ₹ 7.50. This statement is _______.

    (A) True

    (B) False

    (C) Insufficient information

    (D) None of these

15. If Manpreet has ₹ 122 and he wants to buy as many chocolates as he can with this amount. The number of chocolates that he can buy is _______.

    (A) 15

    (B) 20

    (C) 24

    (D) 30

16. Multiply ₹ 435.60 by 12.

(A) ₹ 5227.20

(B) ₹ 6227.20

(C) ₹ 5227

(D) ₹ 5127.01

17. Yuvraj is very fond of reading books. Once he bought books for ₹ 465 and she paid ₹ 500 to the bookstore, which expression shows the correct amount of change that he will get back?

(A) ₹ 500 + ₹ 465

(B) ₹ 500 − ₹ 465

(C) ₹ 500 ÷ ₹ 465

(D) ₹ 500 × ₹ 465

18. Pick the odd one out.

(A) January

(B) July

(C) May

(D) November

19. Today is Monday. After 61 days, it will be __________.

(A) Wednesday

(B) Saturday

(C) Tuesday

(D) Thursday

20. The difference between 7 hours 25 min and 3 hrs 45 min is __________.

(A) 4 hrs 15 min

(B) 4 hrs 65 min

(C) 3 hrs 40 min

(D) 4 hrs 45 min

21. The time from 12 mid night to 12 noon is noted as __________.

(A) am

(B) pm

(C) midnight

(D) day

22. PM means __________.

(A) post meridian

(B) post noon

(C) pre noon

(D) none of these

23. 3 hrs 33 min = __________ min.

(A) 333

(B) 210

(C) 213

(D) 180

24. How many weeks are there in 1 year?

(A) 55

(B) 53

(C) 51

(D) 52

25. The month with neither 31 days nor 30 days is __________.

(A) February

(B) April

(C) November

(D) December

26. What is the weight of marble P?

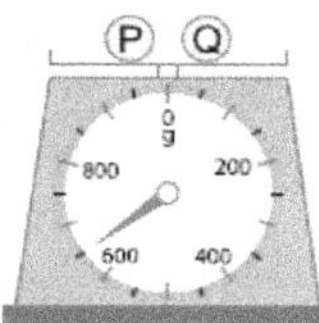 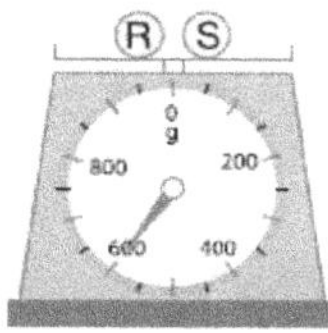 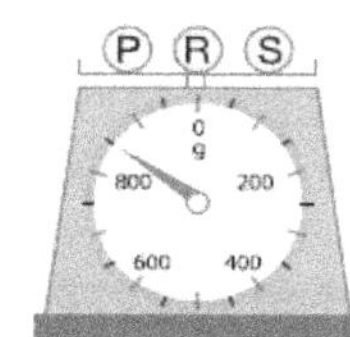

(A) 300 g   (B) 250 g

(C) 240 g   (D) 350 g

27. 4 cups of sugar of the same weight, weigh 520 g. 1 glass of sugar weighs 200 g. How much heavier is 1 glass of sugar than 1 cup of sugar?

(A) 80   (B) 50

(C) 30   (D) 70

28. Sumit went to market to purchase a board game. he gave two coins of ₹ 5, four notes of ₹ 10, three notes of ₹ 50 and two notes of ₹ 500. What is the cost of board game?

(A) ₹ 1500   (B) ₹ 1300

(C) ₹ 1200   (D) ₹ 1000

29. Train A and Train B reach at the station at 9:00 a.m. Train A was early by 30 minutes and Train B was late by 2 hours and 30 minutes. What is the scheduled time of their arrival?

(A) 9:30 a.m., 6:30 a.m.

(B) 9:00 a.m., 7:00 a.m.

(C) 10:00 a.m., 7:30 a.m.

(D) 9:30 a.m., 7:00 a.m.

30. Sahil is going on holiday for 13 days starting from the 11th November, on what day will he come back ?

(A) 24th November

(B) 28th November

(C) 25th November

(D) 21st November

Darken Your Choice with HB Pencil

1.	Ⓐ Ⓑ Ⓒ Ⓓ	7.	Ⓐ Ⓑ Ⓒ Ⓓ	13.	Ⓐ Ⓑ Ⓒ Ⓓ	19.	Ⓐ Ⓑ Ⓒ Ⓓ	25.	Ⓐ Ⓑ Ⓒ Ⓓ
2.	Ⓐ Ⓑ Ⓒ Ⓓ	8.	Ⓐ Ⓑ Ⓒ Ⓓ	14.	Ⓐ Ⓑ Ⓒ Ⓓ	20.	Ⓐ Ⓑ Ⓒ Ⓓ	26.	Ⓐ Ⓑ Ⓒ Ⓓ
3.	Ⓐ Ⓑ Ⓒ Ⓓ	9.	Ⓐ Ⓑ Ⓒ Ⓓ	15.	Ⓐ Ⓑ Ⓒ Ⓓ	21.	Ⓐ Ⓑ Ⓒ Ⓓ	27.	Ⓐ Ⓑ Ⓒ Ⓓ
4.	Ⓐ Ⓑ Ⓒ Ⓓ	10.	Ⓐ Ⓑ Ⓒ Ⓓ	16.	Ⓐ Ⓑ Ⓒ Ⓓ	22.	Ⓐ Ⓑ Ⓒ Ⓓ	28.	Ⓐ Ⓑ Ⓒ Ⓓ
5.	Ⓐ Ⓑ Ⓒ Ⓓ	11.	Ⓐ Ⓑ Ⓒ Ⓓ	17.	Ⓐ Ⓑ Ⓒ Ⓓ	23.	Ⓐ Ⓑ Ⓒ Ⓓ	29.	Ⓐ Ⓑ Ⓒ Ⓓ
6.	Ⓐ Ⓑ Ⓒ Ⓓ	12.	Ⓐ Ⓑ Ⓒ Ⓓ	18.	Ⓐ Ⓑ Ⓒ Ⓓ	24.	Ⓐ Ⓑ Ⓒ Ⓓ	30.	Ⓐ Ⓑ Ⓒ Ⓓ

GEOMETRY

LEARNING OBJECTIVES

➤ Time
➤ Calendar
➤ Money
➤ Important Points about Money

MULTIPLE CHOICE QUESTIONS

1. What do we call a six-sided polygon?
   (A) Heptagon
   (B) Henagon
   (C) Hexagon
   (D) Pentagon

2. How many rectangles are there in the following picture?

   (A) 23
   (B) 24
   (C) 25
   (D) 16

3. Some shapes can be fitted together, edge to edge. This is called _________.
   (A) Paper folding
   (B) Tiling
   (C) Paper cutting
   (D) Tangrams

4. The distance between the centre and any point on the circle is called its.
   (A) Radius
   (B) Diameter
   (C) Circumference
   (D) Area

5. The perimeter of the circle is called its _________.
   (A) Radius
   (B) Diameter
   (C) Circumference
   (D) Centre

6. How many triangles are there in the given figure.

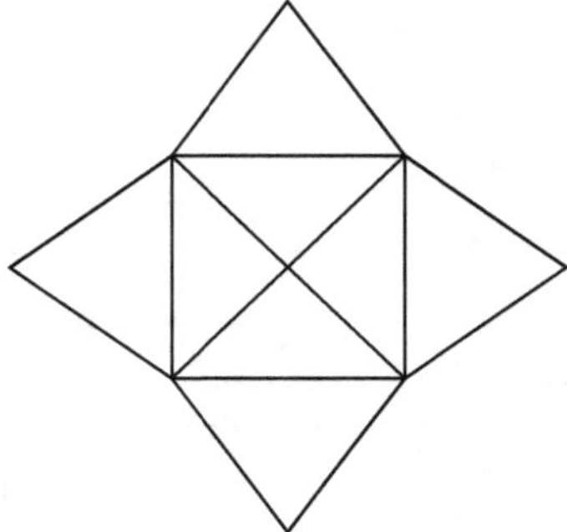

   (A) 15
   (B) 13
   (C) 16
   (D) 12

7. Which of the following dotted liens represents the line of symmetry?

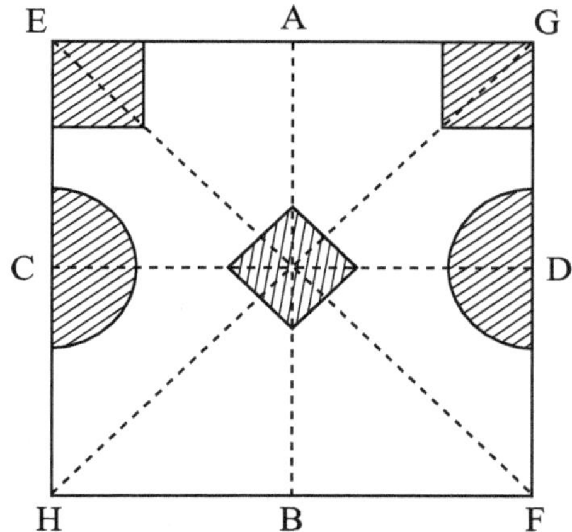

(A) GH   (B) EF
(C) CD   (D) AB

8. What is the perimeter of the given figure?

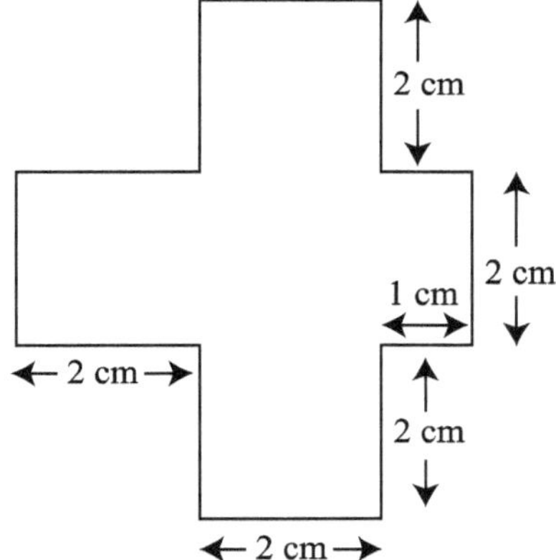

(A) 20 cm
(B) 15 cm
(C) 12 cm
(D) 22 cm

9. Which of the following figures has highest area?

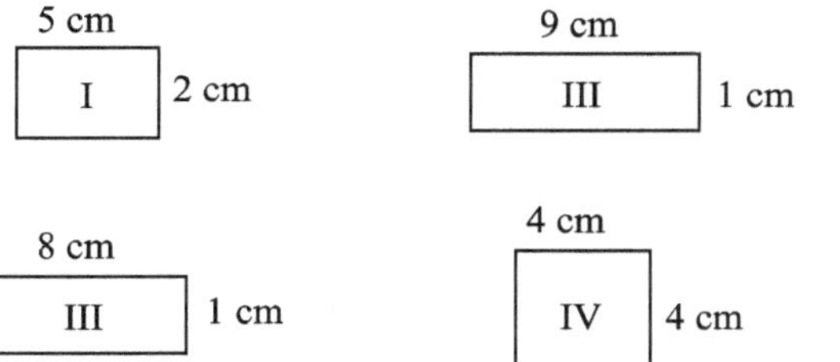

(A) I
(B) II
(C) III
(D) IV

10. Which of the following figures has exactly 3 faces?

(A) 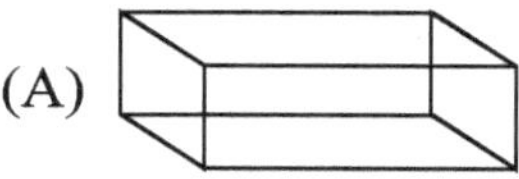

(B) 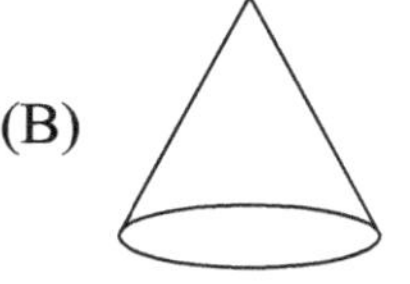

(C) 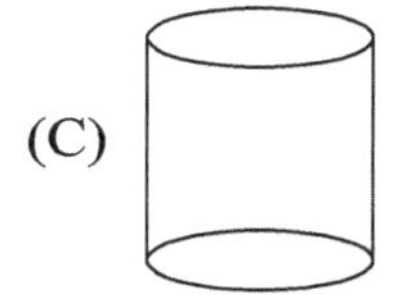

(D) 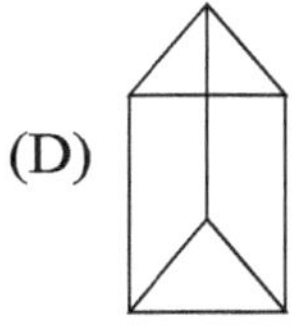

11. Name the figure obtained on joining the given three points.

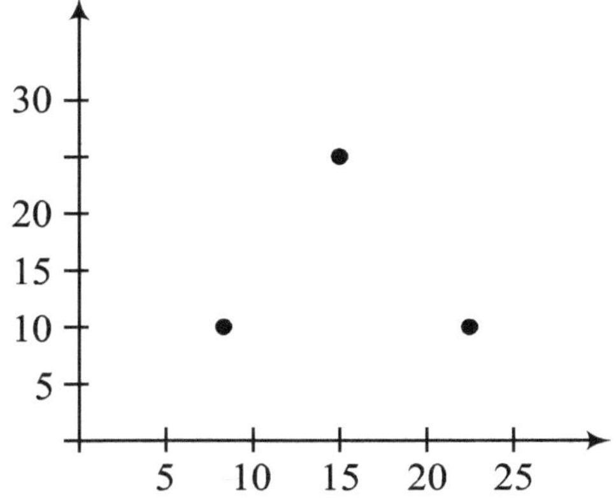

(A) Line
(B) Triangle
(C) Square
(D) Quadrilateral

12. If perimeter of 1 small square is 4 m then what is the area of the whole given figure?

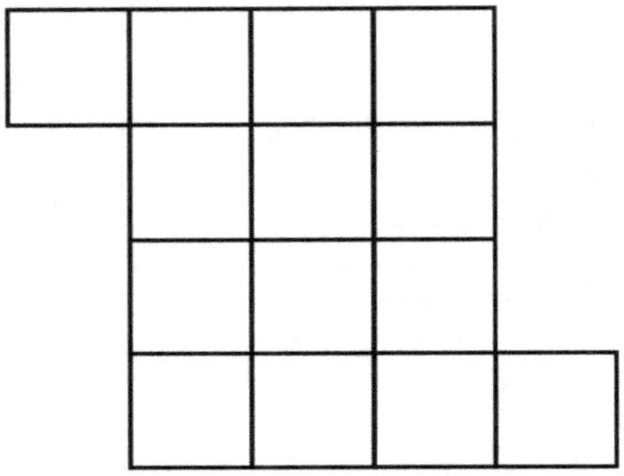

(A) 14 square metre

(B) 15 square metre

(C) 16 square metre

(D) 17 square metre

13. If the side of an equilateral triangle is 10 cm, then find the perimeter of triangle.

(A) 80 cm

(B) 50 cm

(C) 25 cm

(D) 30 cm

14. What is the perimeter of square of side 9 cm?

(A) 35 cm

(B) 36 cm

(C) 37 cm

(D) 38 cm

15. What is the area of 11 unit squares?

(A) 110 square units

(B) 100 square units

(C) 11 square units

(D) 10 square units

16. Metre is the unit of __________.

(A) Area

(B) Volume

(C) Perimeter

(D) Rupees

Direction (17-20): Shraddha is making bedsheets to sell it in the market. She makes bedsheets of different sizes. The table showing size and price of the bedsheet is given below. Read and answer the questions that follow.

S. No.	Bedsheet	Length	Width	Price
1	Small	2 m	1 m	₹ 100
2	Medium	3 m	2 m	₹ 200
3	Large	4 m	3 m	₹ 300
4	Extra large	5 m	4 m	₹ 400
5	Deluxe	6 m	5 m	₹ 500

17. A customer asked for two extra large bedsheets. What is the perimeter of each bedsheet?

(A) 17 m

(B) 18 m

(C) 36 m

(D) 34 m

18. What is the difference between the perimeter of medium bedsheets and deluxe bedsheets?

(A) 10 m

(B) 11 m

(C) 12 m

(D) 13 m

19. A customer asked for 2 small bedsheets, 1 large bedsheet and 2 deluxe bedsheets. How much did he/she have to pay?

(A) ₹ 1000

(B) ₹ 1500

(C) ₹ 2000

(D) ₹ 2500

20. What is the difference between the perimeter of large bedsheet and small bedsheet?

OLYMPIAD WORKBOOK (IMO) CLASS – 4

(A) 5 m

(B) 6 m

(C) 7 m

(D) 8 m

21. Mr. Kumar bought a rectangular field whose length is thrice its breadth. If the breadth of the field is 50 m, find the boundary of the field.

(A) 400 m

(B) 350 m

(C) 450 m

(D) 380 m

22. Neha made a box by folding the given cardboard along the dotted lines. What shape would the box be?

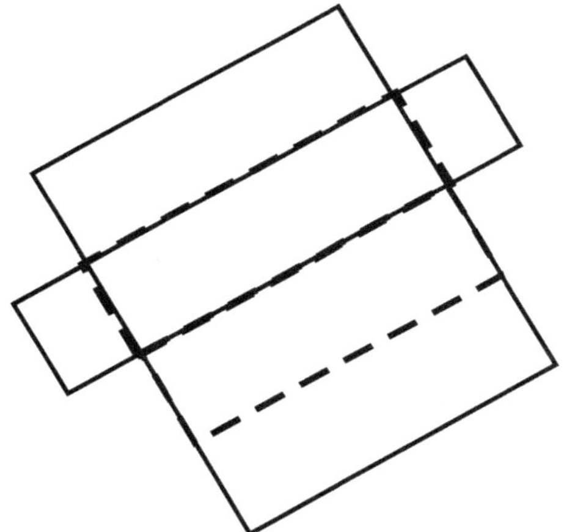

(A) Sphere

(B) Cylinder

(C) Cone

(D) Cuboid

23. Kiran walked along the boundry of a square-shaped park that has 20 m as its side. Rahul walked along the boundary of a rectangular-shaped park that has

20 m × 10 m as its dimension.

Find who walked more.

(A) Rahul

(B) Kiran

(C) Both walked same distance

(D) Cann't say

24. Rohan cut a piece of paper with 5 sides. What is the shape of the paper?

(A) Triangle

(B) Quadrilateral

(C) Square

(D) Pentagon

25. Naina, Shonam, Sohail and Tanu have a circular bangle of radius 2 cm, 3 cm, 5 cm, 1 cm, respectively.

Who has largest bangle?

(A) Sohail

(B) Shonam

(C) Naina

(D) Tanu

26. Which of the given rectangles has the largest perimeter?

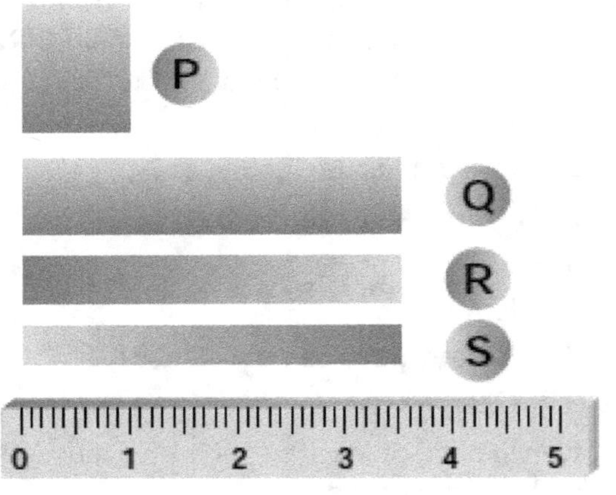

(A) P   (B) Q

(C) R   (D) S

27. There are _________ symmetrical alphabets and _________ non-symmetrical alphabets.

APSERW

(A) 2, 4   (B) 4, 2
(C) 5, 1   (D) 3, 3

28. If 1 ☐ is equal to 1 square unit, then find the figure with greatest perimeter.

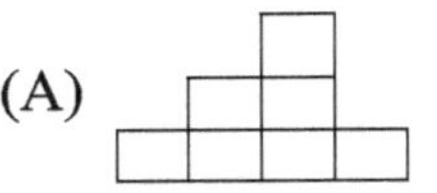
(A)

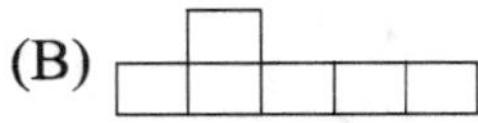
(B)

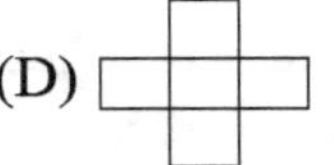
(C)   (D)

29. If side of a square is halved, then the area _________.

(A) Also get halved

(B) Becomes doubled

(C) Becomes one-fourth

(D) Remains the same

30. Identify the unit shape in the tessellation given in the figure.

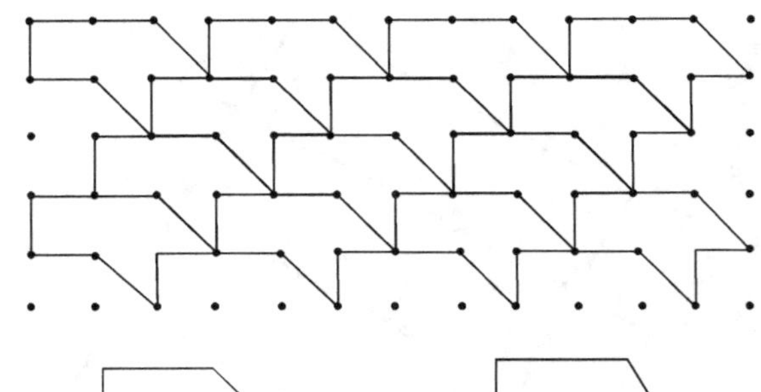

(a)

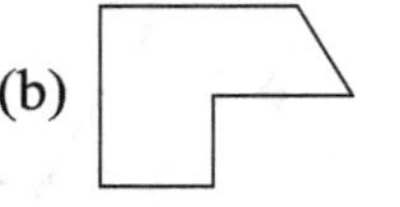
(b)

(c)

(d)

---

1. Ⓐ Ⓑ Ⓒ Ⓓ	7. Ⓐ Ⓑ Ⓒ Ⓓ	13. Ⓐ Ⓑ Ⓒ Ⓓ	19. Ⓐ Ⓑ Ⓒ Ⓓ	25. Ⓐ Ⓑ Ⓒ Ⓓ	
2. Ⓐ Ⓑ Ⓒ Ⓓ	8. Ⓐ Ⓑ Ⓒ Ⓓ	14. Ⓐ Ⓑ Ⓒ Ⓓ	20. Ⓐ Ⓑ Ⓒ Ⓓ	26. Ⓐ Ⓑ Ⓒ Ⓓ	
3. Ⓐ Ⓑ Ⓒ Ⓓ	9. Ⓐ Ⓑ Ⓒ Ⓓ	15. Ⓐ Ⓑ Ⓒ Ⓓ	21. Ⓐ Ⓑ Ⓒ Ⓓ	27. Ⓐ Ⓑ Ⓒ Ⓓ	
4. Ⓐ Ⓑ Ⓒ Ⓓ	10. Ⓐ Ⓑ Ⓒ Ⓓ	16. Ⓐ Ⓑ Ⓒ Ⓓ	22. Ⓐ Ⓑ Ⓒ Ⓓ	28. Ⓐ Ⓑ Ⓒ Ⓓ	
5. Ⓐ Ⓑ Ⓒ Ⓓ	11. Ⓐ Ⓑ Ⓒ Ⓓ	17. Ⓐ Ⓑ Ⓒ Ⓓ	23. Ⓐ Ⓑ Ⓒ Ⓓ	29. Ⓐ Ⓑ Ⓒ Ⓓ	
6. Ⓐ Ⓑ Ⓒ Ⓓ	12. Ⓐ Ⓑ Ⓒ Ⓓ	18. Ⓐ Ⓑ Ⓒ Ⓓ	24. Ⓐ Ⓑ Ⓒ Ⓓ	30. Ⓐ Ⓑ Ⓒ Ⓓ	

DATA HANDLING

LEARNING OBJECTIVES

➤ Point and Line
➤ Types of Line

➤ Plane Shapes
➤ Solid Shapes

MULTIPLE CHOICE QUESTIONS

Direction (1-5): Five boats take visitors out into the sea to watch dolphins swimming. The bar chart shows the number of people that went out on each boat. Read the chart below and answer the questions that follow:

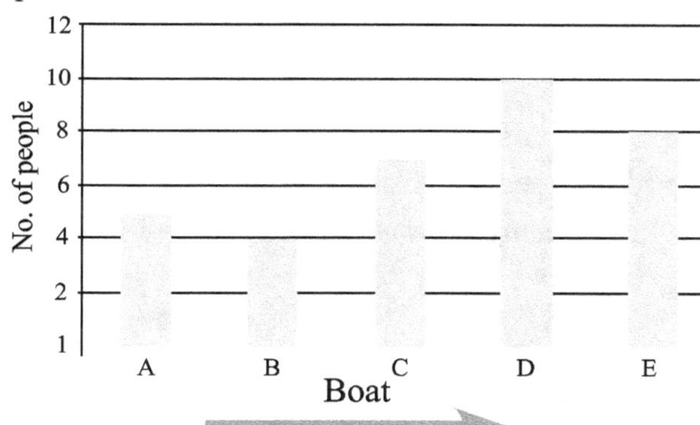

1. If Boat A: 5 :: Boat D : ?
   (A) 4   (B) 5
   (C) 10   (D) 8

2. Find the odd one out.
   (A) Boat A : 5
   (B) Boat B : 4
   (C) Boat C : 8
   (D) Boat E : 8

3. How many more people went to boat D than boat A?
   (A) 5   (B) 4
   (C) 3   (D) 2

4. How many less people went on boat C than boat E?
   (A) 1
   (B) 2
   (C) 3
   (D) 4

5. How many people went all together?
   (A) 31
   (B) 32
   (C) 33
   (D) 34

Directions (6-12): The table given below shows the number of people watching at various football grounds. Round each number to the nearest thousand and put answer in the right column. Then answer the questions that follow.

Team	No. of Players	Rounding
Aryans	2876	3000
Bachelors	6453	6000
Daredevils	3386	3000
Royals	4691	5000
Panthers	9304	9000
Tigers	5771	6000
Shera	6852	7000

6. Which team was watched by most people?

   (A) Bachelors

   (B) Tigers

   (C) Shera

   (D) Panthers

7. Which team was watched by least people?

   (A) Bachelors

   (B) Aryans

   (C) Tigers

   (D) Royals

8. Find the odd one out.

   (A) Tigers

   (B) Aryans

   (C) Cow

   (D) Panthers

9. How many less people watched panthers than Aryans (use rounding)?

   (A) 4000

   (B) 5000

   (C) 6000

   (D) 7000

10. How many less people watched Daredevils than Shera (use rounding)?

   (A) 4000

   (B) 5000

   (C) 6000

   (D) 7000

11. If Tigers : 6000 : : Bachelors : ?

   (A) 5000

   (B) 6000

   (C) 7000

   (D) 8000

12. If Royals : 5000 : : ? : 7000

   (A) Bachelors

   (B) Tigers

   (C) Shera

   (D) Daredevils

Direction (13-19): Golu kept a record of the birds he saw each day for five days. He presented his observation as a pictograph. Read the given pictograph and answer questions that follow.

Types of Bird	Number of Birds
Sparrow	
Seagull	
Pigeon	
Crow	
Parrot	
Bulbul	

1 bird represents 5 birds.

13. How many crows did he see?

   (A) 20

   (B) 25

   (C) 30

   (D) 35

14. How many more pigeons are there than sparrow?

   (A) 40

   (B) 50

   (C) 30

   (D) 20

15. How many fewer parrots are there than seagull?

   (A) 40

   (B) 30

   (C) 20

   (D) 10

16. Which bird was seen as many times as bulbul?

(A) Sparrow

(B) Seagull

(C) Crow

(D) Pigeon

17. State True/false for following.

i. Pigeon was seen more than crow

ii. Bulbul was seen less than seagull.

iii. Sparrow was seen equal times as parrot.

iv. Pigeon was seen more than bulbul.

(A) FTTF

(B) TFFT

(C) FTFT

(D) TFTF

18. Which bird was seen maximum number of times?

(A) Bulbul

(B) Seagull

(C) Crow

(D) Pigeon

19. Which bird was seen minimum number of times?

(A) Parrot

(B) Crow

(C) Bulbul

(D) Sparrow

20. Which of the following statements is/are correct?

i. When we give information (data) about a quantity through pictures, it is called a bar graph

ii. When we give information (data) about a quantity through horizontal or vertical bars, it is called bargraph.

(A) Only i

(B) Only ii

(C) Both i and ii

(D) Neither i nor

HOTS (ACHIEVERS SECTION)

21. The given bar graph shows the height of five children. What is the difference between the height of the tallest child and the shortest child?

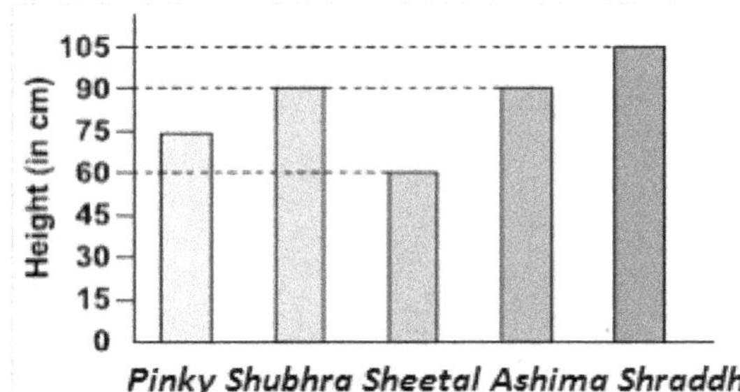

(A) 45 cm

(B) 30 cm

(C) 60 cm

(D) 105 cm

22. Which statement is incorrect for a bar graph?

(A) All bars are of the same width

(B) All bars are unevenly spaced.

(C) Label what each bar graph represents.

(D) Bar graphs are difficult to draw and understand.

23. Look at the given table that shows number of people who joined a comp in various years.

Year	Number of People
2013	320
2014	410
2015	205
2016	225

In which year, the number of people joined the company get halved.

(A) 2013, 2014

(B) 2014, 2015

(C) 2015, 2016

(D) 2016, 2013

24. If 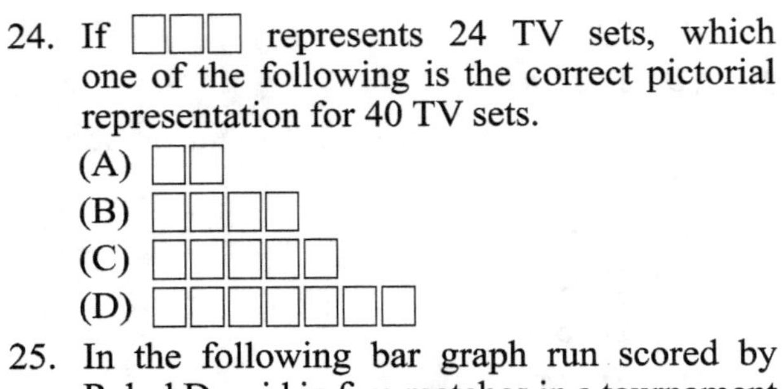 represents 24 TV sets, which one of the following is the correct pictorial representation for 40 TV sets.

(A)

(B)

(C)

(D)

25. In the following bar graph run scored by Rahul Dravid in five matches in a tournament has been shown:

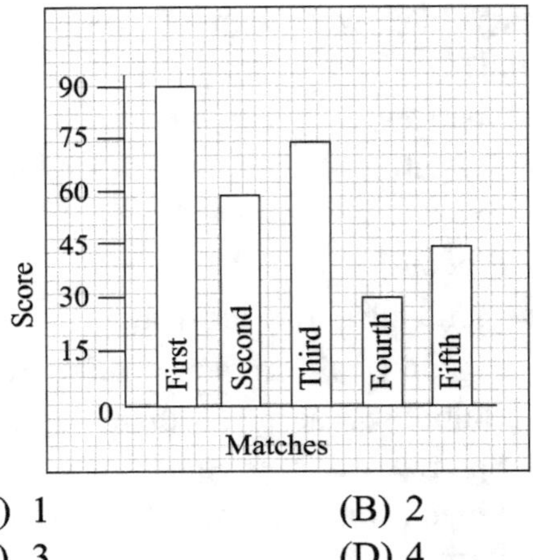

(A) 1   (B) 2
(C) 3   (D) 4

LOGICAL REASONING

7

LEARNING OBJECTIVES

- ➤ Odd One Out
- ➤ Complete the Two Words
- ➤ Matching Pairs
- ➤ Letter Coding
- ➤ Number Coding
- ➤ Number to Letter Coding
- ➤ Number Ranking

- ➤ Alphabet Test
- ➤ Analogy
- ➤ Classification
- ➤ The concept of embedded figures
- ➤ Types of directions
- ➤ Mirror Images of Numbers
- ➤ Mathematical Reasoning

MULTIPLE CHOICE QUESTIONS

1. How many circles will be there in pattern 20?

Pattern 1   Pattern 2

Pattern 3   Pattern 4

(A) 39   (B) 29

(C) 19   (D) 49

2. Which of the following figures will continue the given figure pattern?

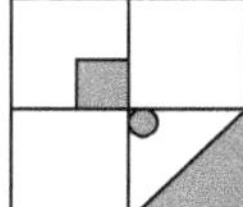   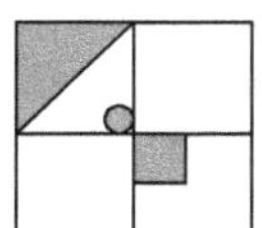   ?

(A) 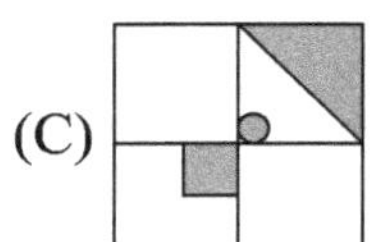   (B) 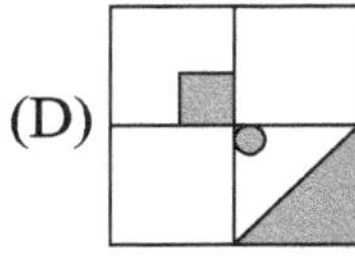

(C)   (D)

3. Which of the following figures will continue the given figure pattern?

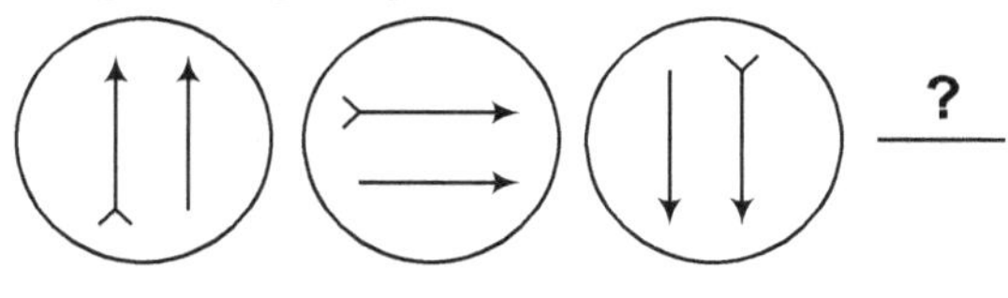   ?

(A) 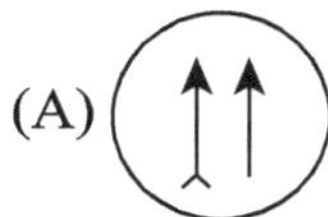   (B) 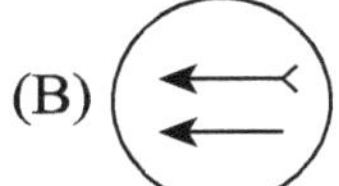

(C) 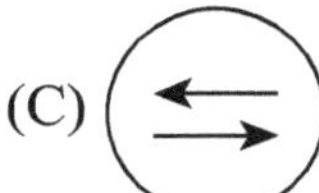   (D) 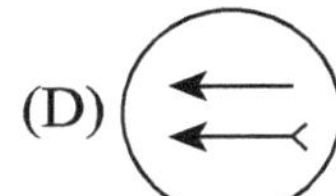

4. If the given matrix follows a certain rule row-wise or column-wise, then find the missing number.

8	4	12
10	15	1
74	?	145

(A) 112
(B) 82
(C) 14
(D) 31

5. Find the missing, if same rule is followed in all the three figures.

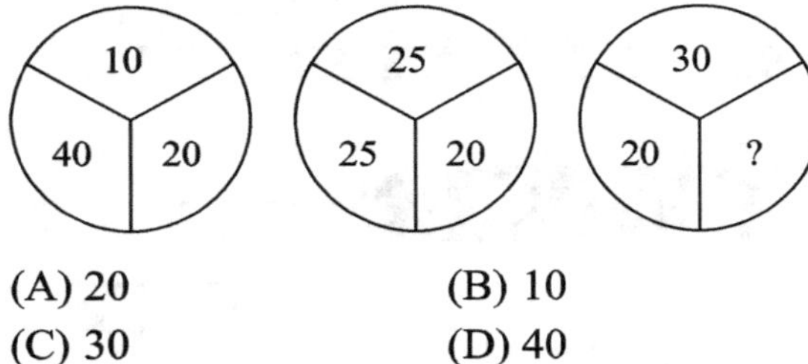

(A) 20
(B) 10
(C) 30
(D) 40

6. Below are given A to Z. Under each capital letter a small letter is written which is to be used as a code for the capital letter.

Letter	A	B	C	D	E	F	G	H	I	J	K	L	M
Code	e	b	n	f	Y	l	h	i	p	a	k	w	v

Letter	N	O	P	Q	R	S	T	U	V	W	X	Y	Z
Code	u	b	z	c	Q	d	o	r	s	t	j	m	G

Group of four capital letters and their equivalent codes are given below.

You have to match each group of capital letters in column I with its code in column II.

Column I	Column II
1. J D R U	(A) a e g i
2. C V F O	(B) a f q r
3. M F H B	(C) n s l b
4. J A Z H	(D) v l i b

(A) 1-B, 2-C, 3-D, 4-A
(B) 1-C, 2-B, 3-D, 4-A
(C) 1-D, 2-C, 3-A, 4-B
(D) None of these

7. If 'Red' is called 'Orange' Orange is called 'Pink' and 'Pink' is called 'Black' what is colour of apple?
(A) Red
(B) Orange
(C) Pink
(D) Black

8. If 'Red' is called 'Pencil', 'Pencil' is called 'Eraser'; 'Eraser' is called 'Notebook', What do we use to erase our mistakes on a notebook?
(A) Pencil
(B) Notebook
(C) Eraser
(D) Pen

9.  If ☐ means △, △ means ◯, ◯ means ⌂ and ⌂ means ◇, then which has no vertex?

(A) ☐
(B) ⌂
(C) ◇
(D) △

10. If 2 means 5, 5 means 9 and 9 means 11, then which is the sum of 2 and 3?
(A) 2
(B) 5
(C) 9
(D) 11

11. In a row of boys, if A who is 10th from the left and B who is 9th from the right interchange their positions, A becomes 15th from the left. How many boys are there in the row?
(A) 23
(B) 31
(C) 127
(D) 28

12. Nilu ranks 18th in a class of 49 students. What is his rank from the last?
(A) 31
(B) 18
(C) 32
(D) 19

13. Raju is sixth from the left end and Viru is tenth from the right end in a row of boys. If there are eight boys between Raju and Viru, how many boys are there in the row?

(A) 24 (B) 26

(C) 23 (D) 25

14. A class of boys stands in a single line. One boy is 19th in order from both the ends. How many boys are there in the class?

(A) 37 (B) 39

(C) 27 (D) 38

15. Sameer ranked 9th from the top and 38th from the bottom in a class. How many students are there in the class ?

(A) 45 (B) 47

(C) 46 (D) 48

16.

(A)

(B)

(C)

(D)

17.

(A)

(B)

(C) 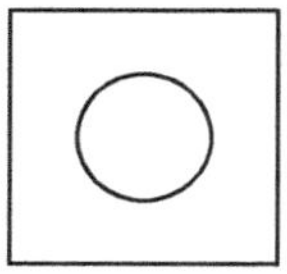

(D) 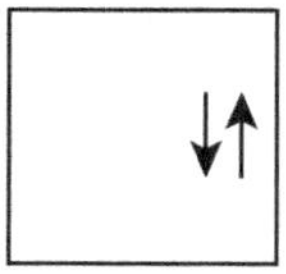

18. 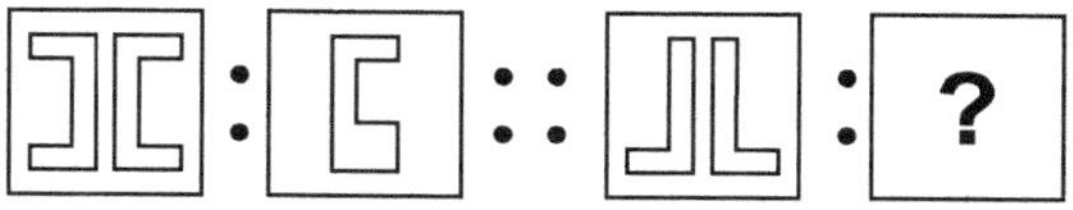

(A) 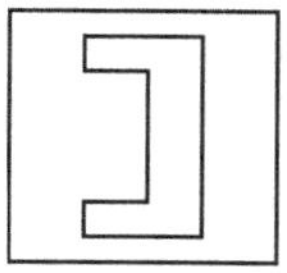

(B) 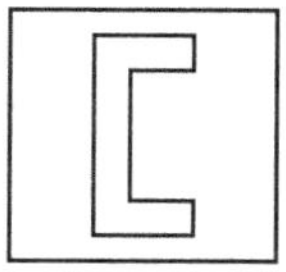

(C) 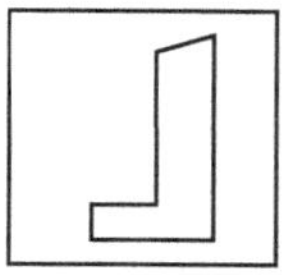

(D) 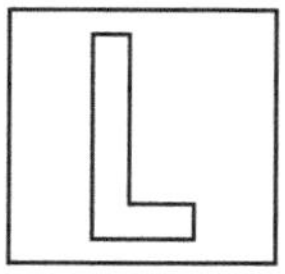

19. 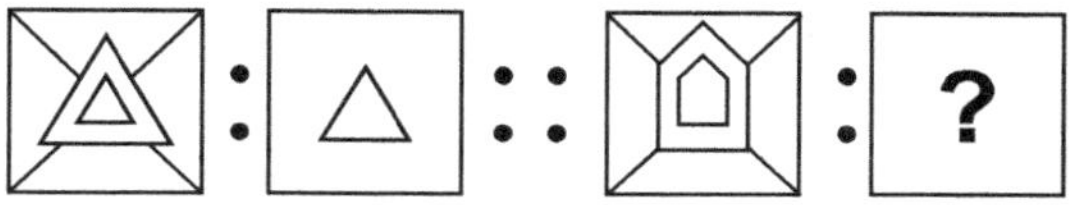

(A) 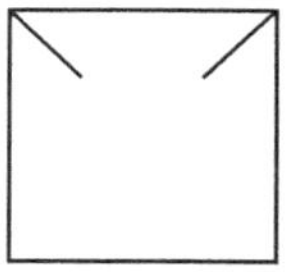

(B) 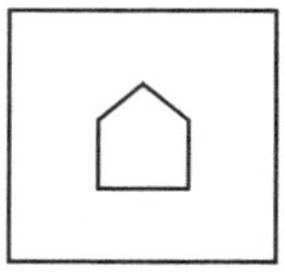

(C) 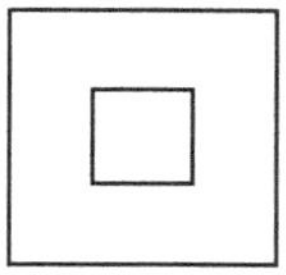

(D) 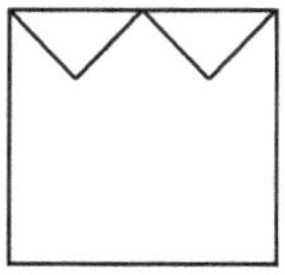

20. 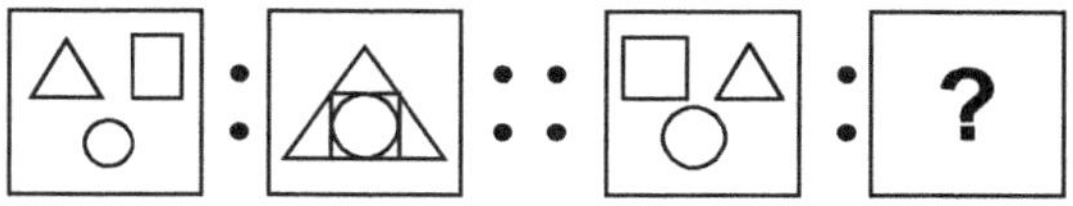

(A) 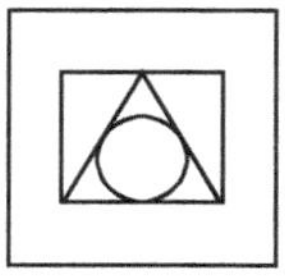

(B) 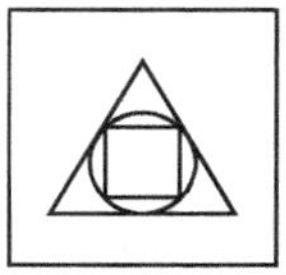

(C) 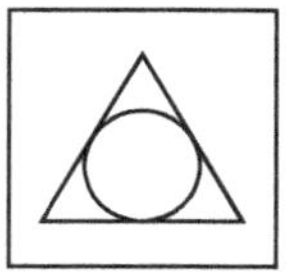

(D) 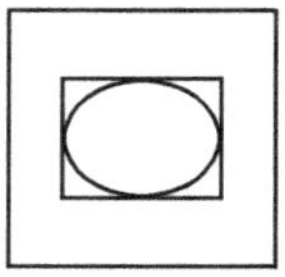

21. 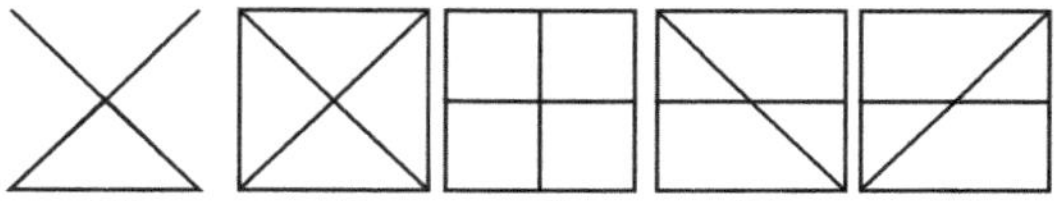

(X) (A) (B) (C) (D)

22. 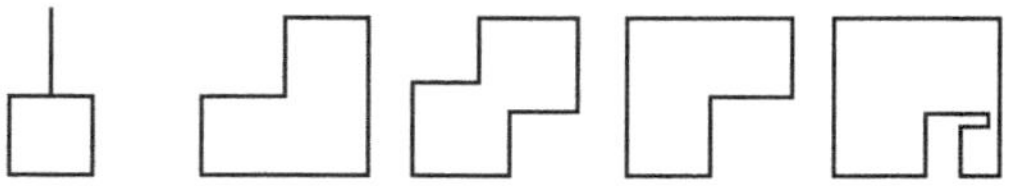

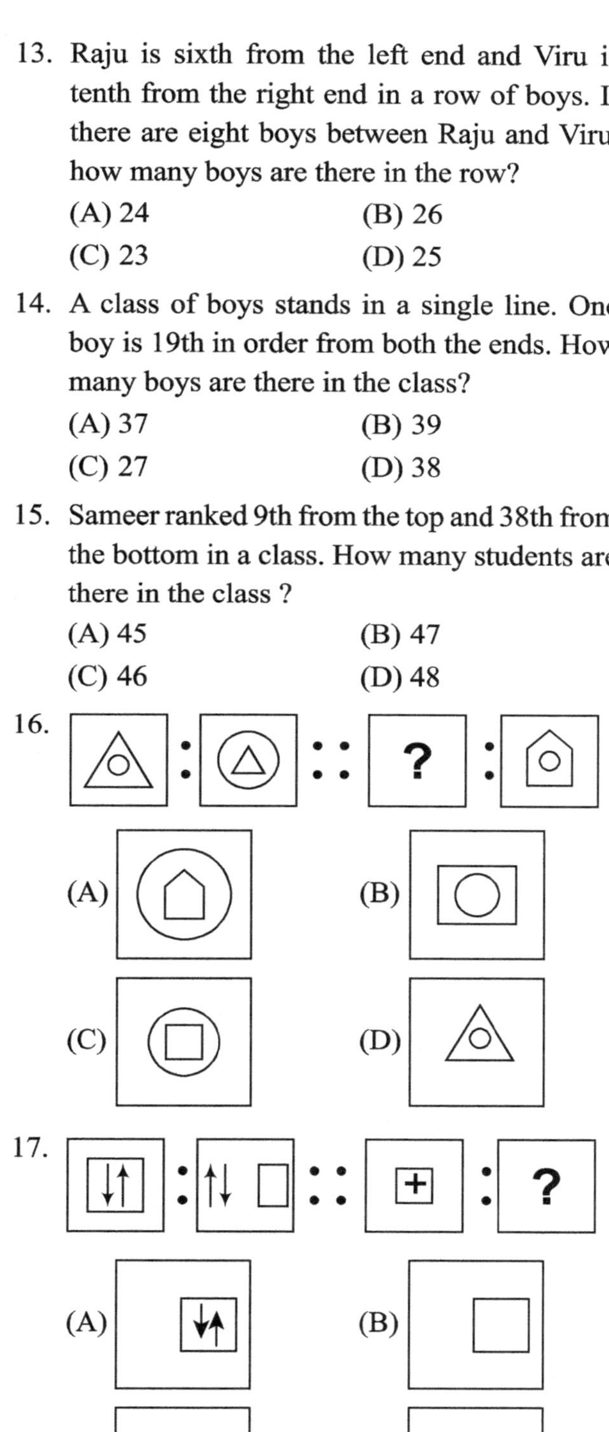

(X) (A) (B) (C) (D)

23.

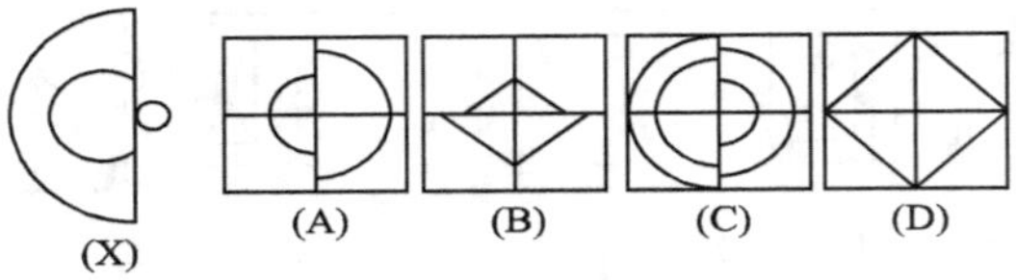

24.

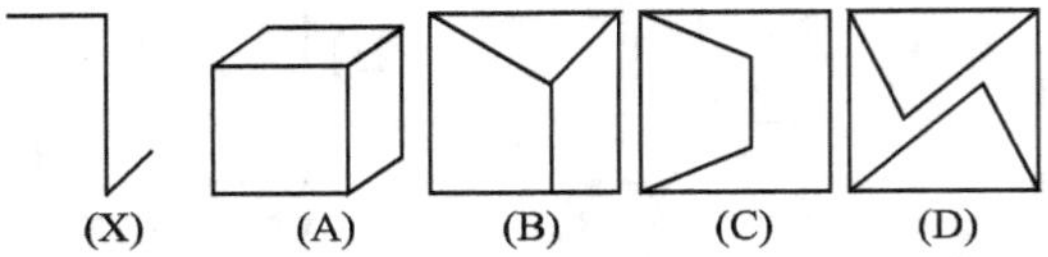

25.

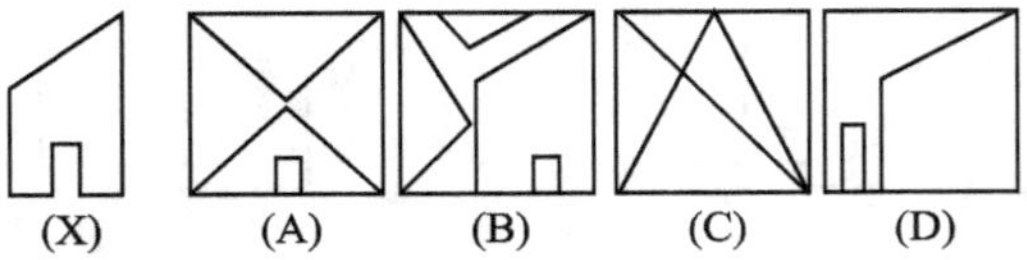

26. Which point is in the South?
(A) X
(B) Y
(C) V
(D) W

27. Which point is in the South-West?
(A) X
(B) Q
(C) U
(D) Y

28. Which point is in the East?
(A) U
(B) W
(C) S
(D) Y

29. Which point is in the West?
(A) W
(B) T
(C) Y
(D) X

30. Which point is in the North-West?
(A) S (B) W
(C) T (D) Z

31. 2 4 7 5 9 6
(A) 6 9 5 7 4 2 (B) ɘ ə ट ٢ ᔨ ƨ
(C) ƨ ᔨ ٢ ट ɘ ə (D) ə ɘ ट ٢ ᔨ ƨ

32. B R 4 A Q 1 6 H I
(A) I H ə 1 Ϙ A ᔨ Я B (B) I H 6 1 Q A ᔨ Я B
(C) I H ə 1 Q A ᔨ Я B (D) I H 9 1 Ϙ A ᔨ Я B

33. G E O G R A P H Y
(A) Y H ꟼ A Я Ɔ O Ǝ Ɔ (B) Y H P A R G O E G
(C) ⅄ H ꟼ A Я Ɔ O Ǝ Ɔ (D) Y H ꟼ Ɐ Я Ɔ O Ǝ Ɔ

34. NATIONAL
(A) ⅃AИOI⊥AИ (B) ⅃AИOITAИ
(C) ⅃ANOITAИ (D) LAИOITAИ

35. PAINTED
(A) ᗡƎTNIAꟼ (B) ᗡƎTИIAꟼ
(C) ᗡƎ⊥ИIAꟼ (D) ᗡETИIAꟼ

36. The total of the ages of Amar, Akbar and Anthony is 80 years. What was the total of their ages three years ago?
(A) 71 years
(B) 72 years
(C) 74 years
(D) 77 years

37. Two bus tickets from city A to B and three tickets from city A to C cost ₹ 77 but three tickets from city A to B and two tickets from city A to C cost ₹ 73. What are the fares for cities B and C from A?
(A) ₹ 4, ₹ 23
(B) ₹ 13, ₹ 17
(C) ₹ 15, ₹ 14
(D) ₹ 17, ₹ 13

38. An institute organised a fete and 1/5 of the girls and 1/8 of the boys participated in the same. What fraction of the total number of students took part in the fete?
(A) 2/13
(B) 13/40
(C) Data inadequate
(D) None of these

39. A number of friends decided to go on a picnic and planned to spend ₹ 96 on eatables. Four of them, however, did not turn up. As a consequence, the remaining ones had to contribute ₹ 4 each extra. The number of those who attended the picnic was _______________.

(A) 8

(B) 12

(C) 16

(D) 24

40. A, B, C, D and E play a game of cards. A says to B, "If you give me three cards, you will have as many as E has and if I give you three cards, you will have as many as D has." A and B together have 10 cards more than what D and E together have. If B has two cards more than what C has and the total number of cards be 133, how many cards does B have?

(A) 22   (B) 23

(C) 25   (D) 35

MULTIPLE CHOICE QUESTIONS

1. How many smiling faces as shown below will there be in Pattern 10?

    Pattern 1   Pattern 2   Pattern 3

(A) 122   (B) 124
(C) 126   (D) 128

2. Observe the series given below.

   1 2 2 3 3 3 4 4 4 4 5 5 5 5 5 .... What is the 20th term of the series?

   (A) 6   (B) 7
   (C) 8   (D) 5

3. Clock I shows the time when Anny starts to draw an apple.

    I   II

Anny takes 20 seconds to draw an apple. What will be the correct position of minute hand and second hand on clock II?

(A) P,R   (B) P,Q
(C) R,S   (D) Q,S

4. Weight of an apple as shown by the balance scale is _________ g.

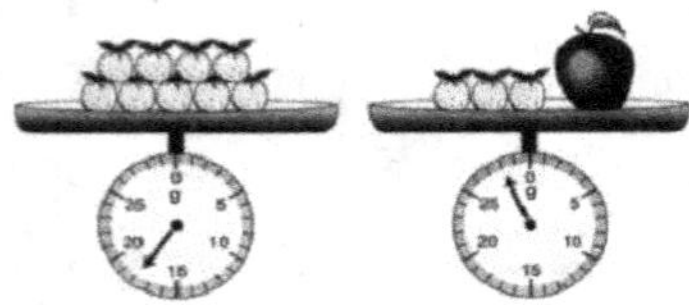

(A) 33   (B) 22
(C) 28   (D) 9

5. Which fraction of the following figure is shaded?

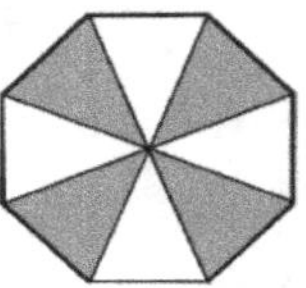

(A) 6/8   (B) 4/8
(C) 3/8   (D) 5/8

6. How many triangles are there in the following figure?

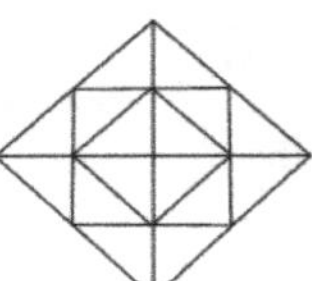

(A) 29   (B) 30
(C) 32   (D) None of these

7. Each ☐ is 1 square unit. ◺ ◿ are equal to ◹. Each ◺ is ½ of a square unit. Then the area of following figure is _________

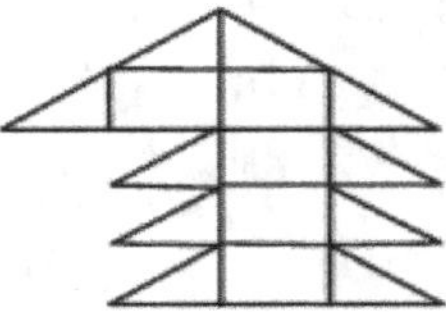

(A) 12 sq. units
(B) 10 sq. units
(C) 8 sq. units.
(D) 11 sq. units.

8. How many meaningful words can be formed by the letters W, N, O using all three letters? If no word is formed, then mark your answer as X and if one word is formed, mark as Y.
(A) 2
(B) 3
(C) Y
(D) X

9. How many meaningful words can be made from the second, third, sixth, seventh and tenth letters of the word 'MEANINGFUL', using each letter once and the words starting with Alphabet 'A'?
(A) 0
(B) 1
(C) 2
(D) 3

10. What is the missing number?

(A) 18
(B) 19
(C) 20
(D) 21

11. Which is the next figure in the pattern given below?

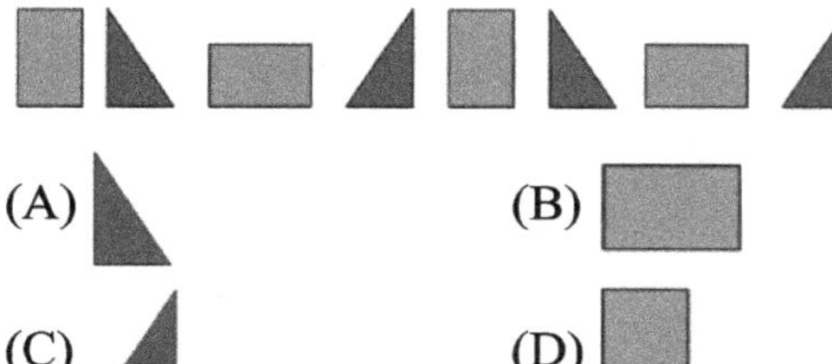

(A) 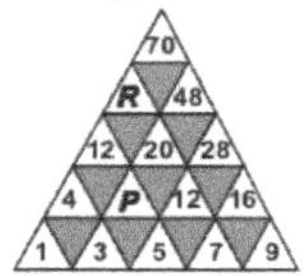
(B)
(C)
(D)

12. The adjoining triangle follows a number pattern.

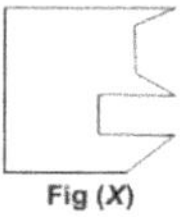

What are the values of P and R?
(A) 22,8
(B) 8,32
(C) 16,8
(D) 8,16

13. Some broken parts of mirrors are shown in the alternatives. Which one of them completes the mirror in Fig (X)?

Fig (X)

(A)
(B)
(C)
(D)

14. Jiya mixed some numbers given in the adjoining box.

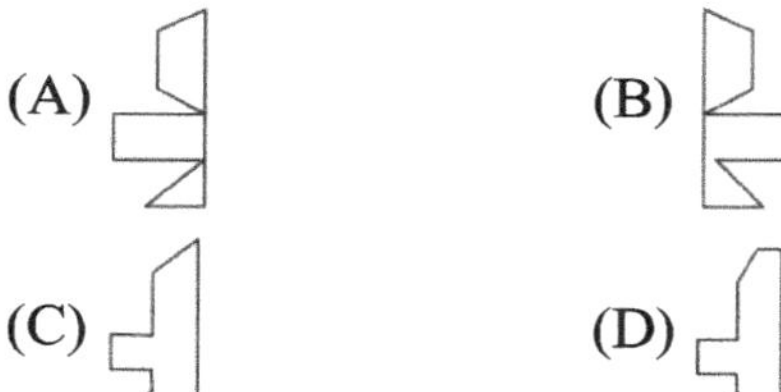

What is the fraction part of 3 among the numbers?
(A) 5/23
(B) 4/22
(C) 5/26
(D) 2/13

15. Rohit has a bag full of 8 red marbles, 4 blue marbles, 5 green marbles and 9 yellow marbles, all of the same size. What is the fraction of red marbles in the bag?
(A) 8/26
(B) 4/26
(C) 5/26
(D) 9/26

16. The diagram given below shows the pattern which Mohit uses to put tiles on his floor. Which column of tiles is missing from Mohit's floor?

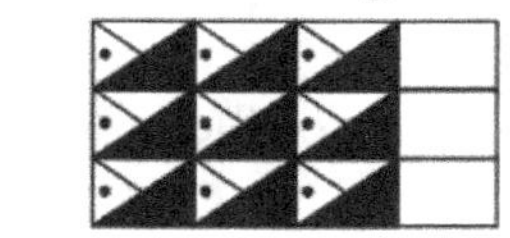

(A) 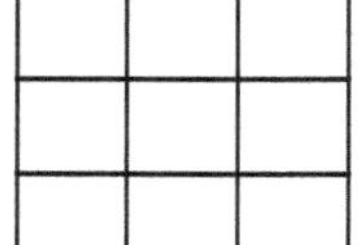
(B)
(C)
(D)

17. Which 2 shapes should be put together to form the square in given figure?

(A) 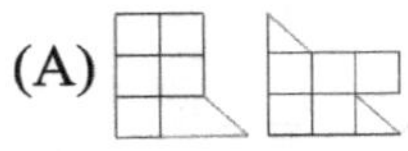

(B) 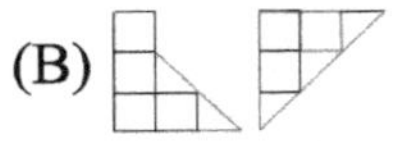

(C) 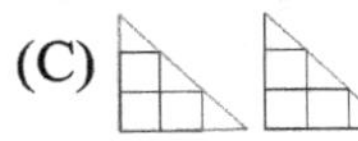

(D) 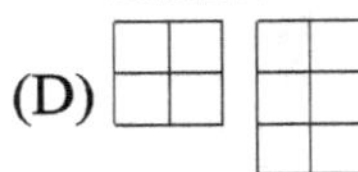

18. Niti rolls a cube which has following shapes on each face.

What is the fraction of symmetric shapes on the cube?

(A) 3/6

(B) 1/5

(C) 5/6

(D) 2/6

19. Sneha used a wire to make the following figure.

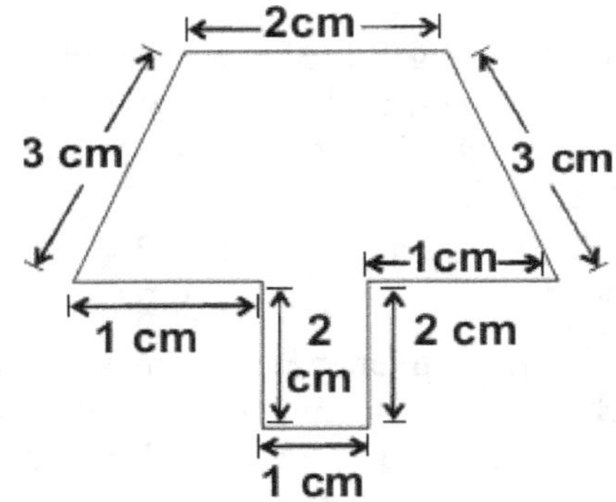

What is the length of the wire?

(A) 15 cm

(B) 12 cm

(C) 13 cm

(D) 14 cm

20. The length of the pencil is __________.

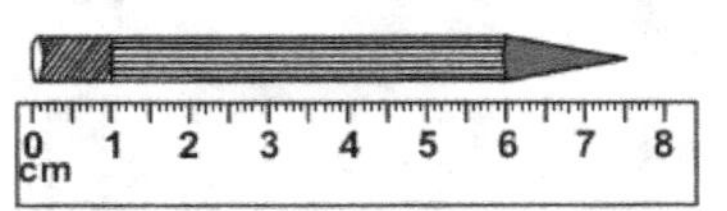

(A) 6 cm

(B) 7 cm

(C) 7.5 cm

(D) 8 cm

21. If 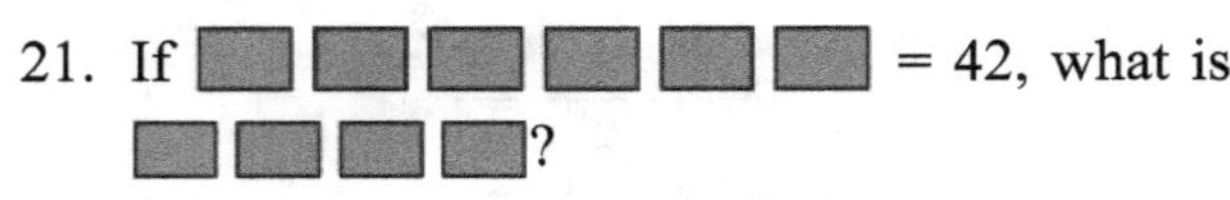 = 42, what is ?

(A) 7

(B) 14

(C) 28

(D) 35

22. Study the number line given below. Fill the correct answer in the boxes.

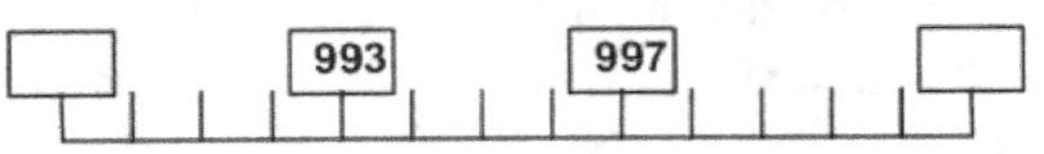

(A) 994, 998

(B) 989, 1001

(C) 990, 1000

(D) 989, 1002

23. If $\diamond \times 4 = \star$, $\star - \diamond = 330$, then what is $\star + \diamond$?

(A) 110

(B) 440

(C) 550

(D) 990

24. If the weight of the papayas is equal, then weight of 1 papaya is __________.

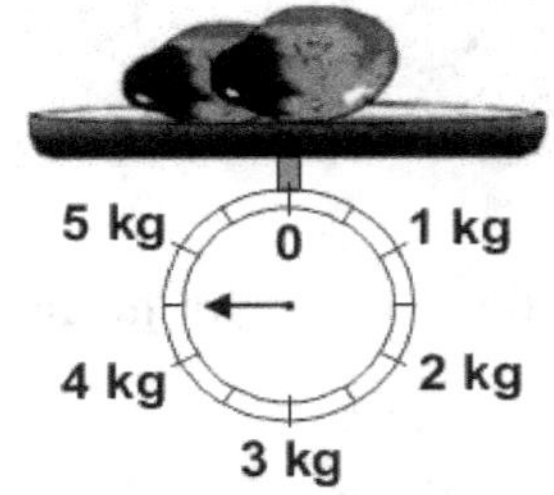

(A) $3\dfrac{1}{4}$ kg

(B) $4\dfrac{1}{4}$ kg

(C) $2\dfrac{1}{4}$ kg

(D) $1\dfrac{1}{4}$ kg

25. Total number of common factors of 48 and 86 is/ are _____

(A) 2

(B) 3

(C) 4

(D) 1

26. The standard numeral for MDCVI is _____

(A) 1606

(B) 1305

(C) 1503

(D) 1402

27. Arrange the sequence given below in ascending order.

1, 2, 2, 5, 4, 3, 9, 8, 7, 1, 3, 4, 5

Which of the following is the sum of middle and last digit?

(A) 13   (B) 12
(C) 11   (D) 15

28. Container B contains _______ water than container C.

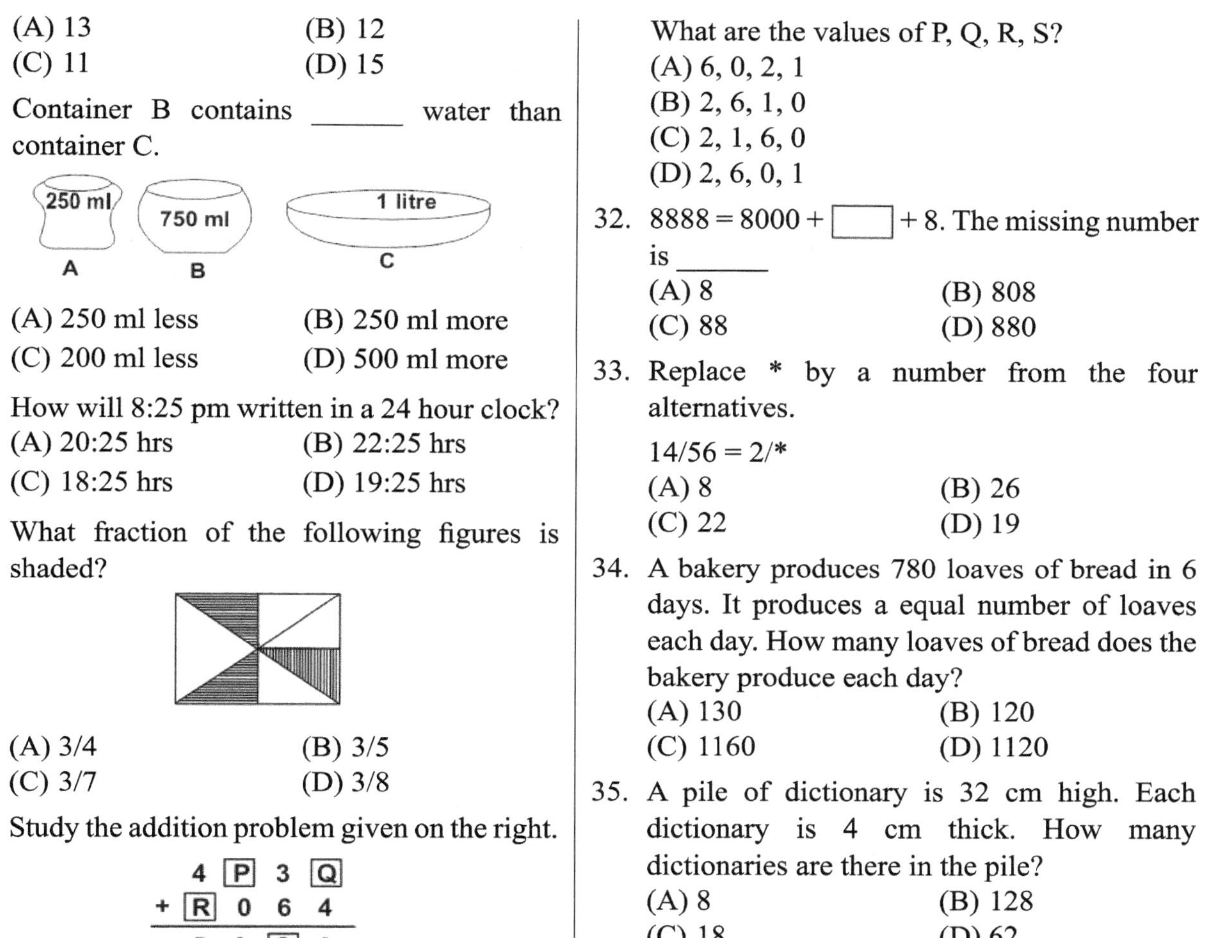

(A) 250 ml less   (B) 250 ml more
(C) 200 ml less   (D) 500 ml more

29. How will 8:25 pm written in a 24 hour clock?
(A) 20:25 hrs   (B) 22:25 hrs
(C) 18:25 hrs   (D) 19:25 hrs

30. What fraction of the following figures is shaded?

(A) 3/4   (B) 3/5
(C) 3/7   (D) 3/8

31. Study the addition problem given on the right.

```
    4 [P] 3 [Q]
  + [R] 0 6  4
  ____________
    5   3 [S] 0
```

What are the values of P, Q, R, S?
(A) 6, 0, 2, 1
(B) 2, 6, 1, 0
(C) 2, 1, 6, 0
(D) 2, 6, 0, 1

32. $8888 = 8000 + \boxed{} + 8$. The missing number is _______
(A) 8   (B) 808
(C) 88   (D) 880

33. Replace * by a number from the four alternatives.

14/56 = 2/*

(A) 8   (B) 26
(C) 22   (D) 19

34. A bakery produces 780 loaves of bread in 6 days. It produces a equal number of loaves each day. How many loaves of bread does the bakery produce each day?
(A) 130   (B) 120
(C) 1160   (D) 1120

35. A pile of dictionary is 32 cm high. Each dictionary is 4 cm thick. How many dictionaries are there in the pile?
(A) 8   (B) 128
(C) 18   (D) 62

Darken Your Choice with HB Pencil

1.	(A) (B) (C) (D)	8.	(A) (B) (C) (D)	15.	(A) (B) (C) (D)	22	(A) (B) (C) (D)	29.	(A) (B) (C) (D)
2.	(A) (B) (C) (D)	9.	(A) (B) (C) (D)	16.	(A) (B) (C) (D)	23.	(A) (B) (C) (D)	30.	(A) (B) (C) (D)
3.	(A) (B) (C) (D)	10.	(A) (B) (C) (D)	17.	(A) (B) (C) (D)	24.	(A) (B) (C) (D)	31.	(A) (B) (C) (D)
4.	(A) (B) (C) (D)	11.	(A) (B) (C) (D)	18.	(A) (B) (C) (D)	25.	(A) (B) (C) (D)	32.	(A) (B) (C) (D)
5.	(A) (B) (C) (D)	12.	(A) (B) (C) (D)	19.	(A) (B) (C) (D)	26.	(A) (B) (C) (D)	33.	(A) (B) (C) (D)
6.	(A) (B) (C) (D)	13.	(A) (B) (C) (D)	20.	(A) (B) (C) (D)	27.	(A) (B) (C) (D)	34.	(A) (B) (C) (D)
7.	(A) (B) (C) (D)	14.	(A) (B) (C) (D)	21.	(A) (B) (C) (D)	28.	(A) (B) (C) (D)	35.	(A) (B) (C) (D)

HINTS AND SOLUTIONS

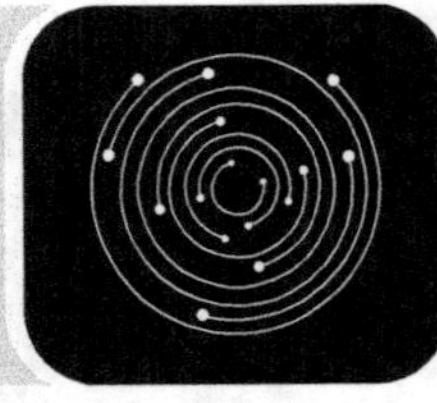

1. NUMBERS SENSE

Answer Key

1. (A)	2. (A)	3. (B)	4. (A)	5. (A)	6. (A)	7. (A)	8. (D)	9. (A)	10. (C)
11. (B)	12. (B)	13. (D)	14. (A)	15. (D)	16. (A)	17. (B)	18. (A)	19. (B)	20. (C)
21. (B)	22. (D)	23. (B)	24. (C)	25. (B)					

1. (A)

Greatest 5-digit number = 99999

2. (A)

Place value of 5 in 5,43,621

$= 5 \times 100,000 = 500000$

3. (B)

Smallest 6-digit number = 1,00,000

4. (A)

We have $300000 + 20000 + 4000 + 200 + 2$

=	L	TTh	T	H	T	O
	3	0	0	0	0	0
	0	2	0	0	0	0
	0	0	4	0	0	0
	0	0	0	2	0	0
+	0	0	0	0	0	2
	3	2	4	2	0	2

9. (A)

We use comma to separate the periods.

13. (D)

All are 6-digit numbers except 23,456.

16. (A)

3,44,567 has 3 lakhs.since

L	TTh	T	H	T	O
3	4	4	5	6	7

HOTS (ACHIEVERS SECTION)

26. (C)	27. (A)	28. (B)	29. (A)	30. (B)

2. COMPUTATION OPERATION

Answer Key

1. (A)	2. (A)	3. (A)	4. (D)	5. (D)	6. (A)	7. (A)	8. (B)	9. (A)	10. (B)
11. (C)	12. (A)	13. (D)	14. (A)	15. (C)	16. (B)	17. (A)	18. (D)	19. (C)	20. (D)
21. (D)	22. (A)	23. (D)	24. (D)	25. (A)					

4. (D)

Here, V = 5, IV = 4, X = 10, XI = 11
But VIIII is meaningless.

5. (D)

N is meaningless in roman numbers.

7. (A)

If we change the order of the numbers being added, the sum does not change. (Property of addition) i.e., $a + b = b + a$

9. (A)

If we add zero to any number, the sum remains the same (Property of addition)

11. (C)

The result after subtraction is called difference.

13. (D)

Clearly, the sum is different.

15. (C)

Multiplication is the short form of repeated addition.

16. (B) We know $43243 \times 0 = 0$

18. (D)

When we share equally, we divide.

19. (C)

After dividing a number, the left over is called remainder.

22. (A)

Clearly 5 is a factor of 45 and not a multiple of 3.

23. (D)

26, 39 and 65 are multiples of 13.

24. (D)

Clearly 48, 64 and 80 are multiples of 16 between 40 and 90.

HOTS (ACHIEVERS SECTION)

26. (A)	27. (D)	28. (A)	29. (C)	30. (C)

3. FRACTIONS

Answer Key

1. (D)	2. (D)	3. (C)	4. (A)	5. (B)	6. (B)	7. (C)	8. (A)	9. (C)	10. (C)
11. (C)	12. (A)	13. (C)	14. (A)	15. (C)	16. (D)	17. (A)	18. (A)	19. (C)	20. (B)
21. (A)	22. (A)	23. (C)	24. (C)	25. (C)					

1. (D)

$\dfrac{21}{5}$ is not a proper fraction.

2. (D)

$\dfrac{31}{8} = 3\dfrac{7}{8} = 3\left(\dfrac{7}{8}\right)$

3. (C)

$\dfrac{A}{B} = 1$ is possible when $a = b$

6. (B)

$\dfrac{4}{3} = 1.3$ and $\dfrac{8}{6} = 1.3$

Hence, $\dfrac{4}{3}$ and $\dfrac{8}{6}$ are equivalent.

8. (A)

$\dfrac{2}{3}$ of an hour $= \dfrac{2}{3} \times 60$ minutes $= 40$ minutes

9. (C)

Here, $\dfrac{1}{3}+\dfrac{1}{6}+\dfrac{1}{12}=X$

then $\dfrac{4+2+1}{12}=X \Rightarrow X=\dfrac{7}{12}$

$\therefore \quad \dfrac{17}{12}+X=\dfrac{17}{12}+\dfrac{7}{12}=\dfrac{24}{12}=2$

12. (A)

We have $\dfrac{9}{15}=\dfrac{\frac{9}{3}}{\frac{15}{3}}=\dfrac{3}{5}$

13. (C) We have $\dfrac{2}{5}\times\dfrac{3}{4}\times\dfrac{5}{8}=\dfrac{3}{16}$

22. (A) Required no. of people $=\dfrac{20}{4}=5$

HOTS (ACHIEVERS SECTION)				
26. (B)	27. (A)	28. (C)	29. (D)	30. (A)

4. MEASUREMENTS, TIME, CALENDERS AND MONEY

Answer Key

1. (C)	2. (C)	3. (D)	4. (B)	5. (D)	6. (A)	7. (B)	8. (D)	9. (B)	10. (C)
11. (B)	12. (B)	13. (C)	14. (B)	15. (C)	16. (A)	17. (B)	18. (D)	19. (B)	20. (C)
21. (A)	22. (A)	23. (C)	24. (D)	25. (A)					

1. (C)

2 is the tallest Giraffe.

2. (C)

Required height $= 620 - 438 = 182$ cm

10. (C) Cost of 2 pens $=$ ₹ 24

Cost of 1 pen $=$ ₹ 24/2 $=$ ₹ 12

So, cost of 5 pens $=$ ₹ 12 $\times$ 5 $=$ ₹ 60

11. (B)

Sum:
$$\begin{array}{r} 150.60 \\ +\,140.75 \\ \hline 291.35 \end{array}$$

Difference:
$$\begin{array}{r} 325.50 \\ 291.35 \\ \hline 33.15 \end{array}$$

12. (B)

Total amount Ankit needs to pay

$$= \dfrac{180}{2}+\dfrac{15}{3}=90+5=95$$

14. (B)

Price of two chocolates $=\dfrac{15}{3}\times 2=10$

Hence, given statement is not correct.

15. (C)

Price of one chocolate $=\dfrac{15}{3}=5$

$\therefore$ Manpreet can buy $=\dfrac{122}{5}$

$$= 24 \text{ chocolates} + 2$$

18. (D)

Month	No. of days
January	31
May	31
July	31
November	30

19. (B)

$$61 \text{ days} = \frac{61}{7} = 8 \text{ weeks} + 5 \text{ days}$$

If today is Monday, then after 61 days
= Monday + 5 days
= Saturday

21. (A)
The time for 12 mid night to 12 noon is noted as am.

22. (A)
PM = Post meridian

24. (D)
1 Year = 52 weeks + 1 day

<table>
<tr><td colspan="5">HOTS (ACHIEVERS SECTION)</td></tr>
<tr><td>26. (B)</td><td>27. (D)</td><td>28. (C)</td><td>29. (A)</td><td>30. (A)</td></tr>
</table>

5. GEOMETRY

Answer Key

1. (C)	2. (D)	3. (B)	4. (A)	5. (C)	6. (D)	7. (D)	8. (D)	9. (D)	10. (B)
11. (B)	12. (A)	13. (D)	14. (B)	15. (C)	16. (C)	17. (B)	18. (C)	19. (B)	20. (D)
21. (A)	22. (D)	23. (B)	24. (D)	25. (A)					

1. (C)
Six-sided polygon is called hexagon.

4. (A)
The distance between the centre and any point on the circle is called its (diameter/2) radius.

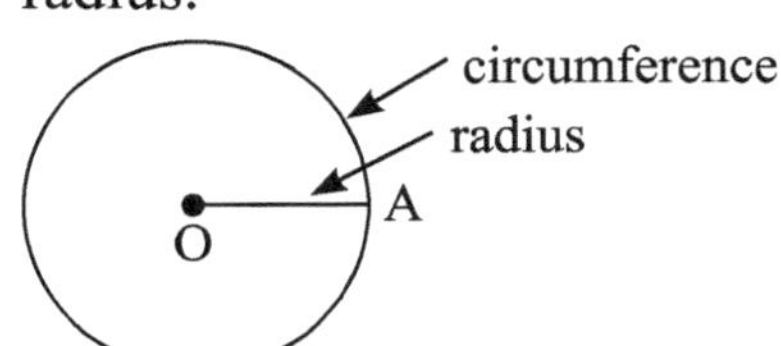

5. (C)
The perimeter of the circle is called its circumference.

14. (B)
Perimeter of square = 4 × side
= 4 × 9 = 36 cm

16. (C)
Perimeter is measured in metre.

17. (B)
Perimeter of sheet = 2{4 + 5} = 2 × 9 = 18 m

<table>
<tr><td colspan="5">HOTS (ACHIEVERS SECTION)</td></tr>
<tr><td>26. (B)</td><td>27. (D)</td><td>28. (A)</td><td>29. (C)</td><td>30. (A)</td></tr>
</table>

30. (A)
The unit shape that gives the tessellation is 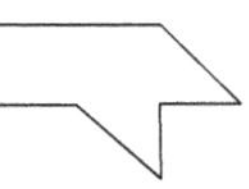 as in option (A)

Answer Key

1. (C)	2. (C)	3. (A)	4. (A)	5. (D)	6. (D)	7. (B)	8. (C)	9. (C)	10. (A)
11. (B)	12. (C)	13. (C)	14. (D)	15. (D)	16. (B)	17. (B)	18. (D)	19. (A)	20. (B)

1. (C)

Boat A = 5 then boat D = 10

2. (C)

Clearly Boat C : 7 Hence, C is odd one out.

3. (A)

Required people = 10 − 5 = 5

4. (A)

Required people = 8 − 7 = 1

5. (D)

Total No. of people
$$= 5 + 4 + 7 + 10 + 8 = 34$$

20. (B)

Only statement 2 is correct.

HOTS (ACHIEVERS SECTION)

1. (A)	2. (B)	3. (B)	4. (C)	5. (C)

7. LOGICAL REASONING

Answer Key

1. (A)	2. (C)	3. (D)	4. (D)	5. (A)	6. (A)	7. (B)	8. (B)	9. (B)	10. (C)
11. (A)	12. (C)	13. (A)	14. (A)	15. (C)	16. (A)	17. (B)	18. (D)	19. (B)	20. (A)
21. (A)	22. (B)	23. (C)	24. (A)	25. (B)	26. (C)	27. (C)	28. (B)	29. (D)	30. (C)
31. (D)	32. (A)	33. (A)	34. (B)	35. (B)	36. (A)	37. (B)	38. (B)	39. (A)	40. (C)

12. (A)

Nilu's ranks from the last
$$= (49 − 18) + 1 = 31 + 1 = 32$$

14. (A)

Total No. of boys in the class
$$= 19 + 19 − 1 = 38 − 1 = 37$$

16. (A)

So,

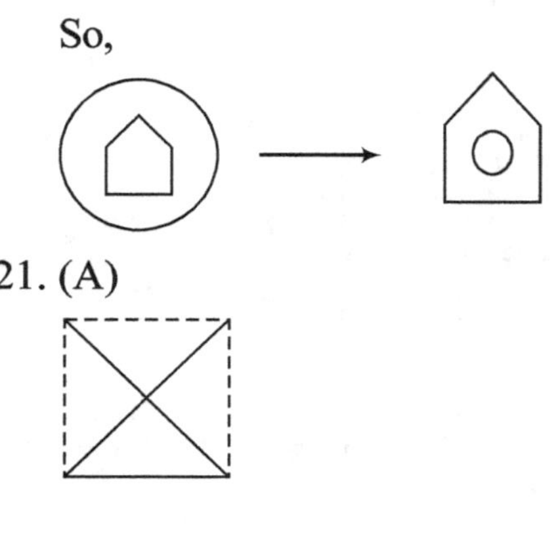

21. (A)

23. (C)

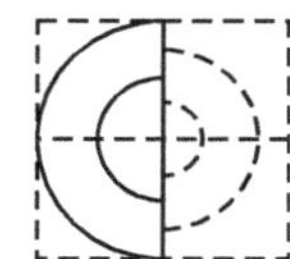

36. (A)

Required sum of ages = $(80 - 3 \times 3)$ years
= $(80 - 9)$ years = 71 years

37. (B)

Let ₹ x be the fare of city B from city A and ₹ y be the fare of city C from city A.

Then, $2x + 3y = 77$ ...(i)

$3x + 2y = 73$ ...(ii)

Multiplying (i) by 3 and (ii) by 2 and subtracting, we get: $5y = 85$ or $y = 17$.

Putting $y = 17$ in (i), we get: $x = 13$.

40. (C)

According to question

$B - 3 = E$ ...(i)

$B + 3 = D$ ...(ii)

MODEL TEST PAPER

Answer Key

1. (A)	2. (A)	3. (B)	4. (D)	5. (B)	6. (D)	7. (B)	8. (B)	9. (C)	10. (B)
11. (D)	12. (B)	13. (A)	14. (C)	15. (A)	16. (A)	17. (C)	18. (C)	19. (A)	20. (C)
21. (C)	22. (B)	23. (C)	24. (C)	25. (A)	26. (A)	27. (A)	28. (D)	29. (A)	30. (C)
31. (B)	32. (D)	33. (A)	34. (A)	35. (A)					

SAMPLE OMR ANSWER SHEET

1. STUDENT NAME (IN ENGLISH CAPITAL LETTERS ONLY)

Students must write and darken the respective circles completely using HB Pencil only. Othewise their Answer Sheets will not be evaluated.

PERSONAL DETAILS

2. SCHOOL CODE

3. CLASS

4. SECTION

5. ROLL NO.

6. QUESTION PAPER SET

A ◯
B ◯
C ◯
D ◯

7. MOBILE NUMBER

8. GENDER

MALE ◯

FEMALE ◯

9. STREAM
(Only for Class XI and XII Students)

MATHEMATICS ◯
BIOLOGY ◯
OTHERS ◯

MARK YOUR ANSWERS

No.	A	B	C	D		No.	A	B	C	D
1.	Ⓐ	Ⓑ	Ⓒ	Ⓓ		26.	Ⓐ	Ⓑ	Ⓒ	Ⓓ
2.	Ⓐ	Ⓑ	Ⓒ	Ⓓ		27.	Ⓐ	Ⓑ	Ⓒ	Ⓓ
3.	Ⓐ	Ⓑ	Ⓒ	Ⓓ		28.	Ⓐ	Ⓑ	Ⓒ	Ⓓ
4.	Ⓐ	Ⓑ	Ⓒ	Ⓓ		29.	Ⓐ	Ⓑ	Ⓒ	Ⓓ
5.	Ⓐ	Ⓑ	Ⓒ	Ⓓ		30.	Ⓐ	Ⓑ	Ⓒ	Ⓓ
6.	Ⓐ	Ⓑ	Ⓒ	Ⓓ		31.	Ⓐ	Ⓑ	Ⓒ	Ⓓ
7.	Ⓐ	Ⓑ	Ⓒ	Ⓓ		32.	Ⓐ	Ⓑ	Ⓒ	Ⓓ
8.	Ⓐ	Ⓑ	Ⓒ	Ⓓ		33.	Ⓐ	Ⓑ	Ⓒ	Ⓓ
9.	Ⓐ	Ⓑ	Ⓒ	Ⓓ		34.	Ⓐ	Ⓑ	Ⓒ	Ⓓ
10.	Ⓐ	Ⓑ	Ⓒ	Ⓓ		35.	Ⓐ	Ⓑ	Ⓒ	Ⓓ
11.	Ⓐ	Ⓑ	Ⓒ	Ⓓ		36.	Ⓐ	Ⓑ	Ⓒ	Ⓓ
12.	Ⓐ	Ⓑ	Ⓒ	Ⓓ		37.	Ⓐ	Ⓑ	Ⓒ	Ⓓ
13.	Ⓐ	Ⓑ	Ⓒ	Ⓓ		38.	Ⓐ	Ⓑ	Ⓒ	Ⓓ
14.	Ⓐ	Ⓑ	Ⓒ	Ⓓ		39.	Ⓐ	Ⓑ	Ⓒ	Ⓓ
15.	Ⓐ	Ⓑ	Ⓒ	Ⓓ		40.	Ⓐ	Ⓑ	Ⓒ	Ⓓ
16.	Ⓐ	Ⓑ	Ⓒ	Ⓓ		41.	Ⓐ	Ⓑ	Ⓒ	Ⓓ
17.	Ⓐ	Ⓑ	Ⓒ	Ⓓ		42.	Ⓐ	Ⓑ	Ⓒ	Ⓓ
18.	Ⓐ	Ⓑ	Ⓒ	Ⓓ		43.	Ⓐ	Ⓑ	Ⓒ	Ⓓ
19.	Ⓐ	Ⓑ	Ⓒ	Ⓓ		44.	Ⓐ	Ⓑ	Ⓒ	Ⓓ
20.	Ⓐ	Ⓑ	Ⓒ	Ⓓ		45.	Ⓐ	Ⓑ	Ⓒ	Ⓓ
21.	Ⓐ	Ⓑ	Ⓒ	Ⓓ		46.	Ⓐ	Ⓑ	Ⓒ	Ⓓ
22.	Ⓐ	Ⓑ	Ⓒ	Ⓓ		47.	Ⓐ	Ⓑ	Ⓒ	Ⓓ
23.	Ⓐ	Ⓑ	Ⓒ	Ⓓ		48.	Ⓐ	Ⓑ	Ⓒ	Ⓓ
24.	Ⓐ	Ⓑ	Ⓒ	Ⓓ		49.	Ⓐ	Ⓑ	Ⓒ	Ⓓ
25.	Ⓐ	Ⓑ	Ⓒ	Ⓓ		50.	Ⓐ	Ⓑ	Ⓒ	Ⓓ

Signature of the Student & Date of Examination

Signature of the Invigilator & Date of Examination

V&S Publishers, F-2/16 Ansari Road, Daryaganj, New Delhi-110002, ☎ 011-23240026-27
✉ info@vspublishers.com, 🌐 www.vspublishers.com